THE NEW DEAL

The New Deal

FIONA VENN

FITZROY
DEARBORN

PUBLISHERS

To my New Deal students,
past, present and future

© Fiona Venn, 1998

Published in the United Kingdom by Edinburgh University Press
22 George Square, Edinburgh

Published in the United States of America by Fitzroy Dearborn Publishers
70 East Walton Street, Chicago, Illinois 60611

Typeset in Monotype Fournier
by Bibliocraft, Dundee, and
printed and bound in Great Britain
by the Cromwell Press, Trowbridge, Wilts

A CIP record for this book is available
from the British Library

A Cataloging-in-Publication record for this book is available
from the Library of Congress

ISBN 1-57958-145-5 Fitzroy Dearborn

Contents

Abbreviations

AAA   Agricultural Adjustment Administration
AFL   American Federation of Labor
CCC   Civilian Conservation Corps *or* Commodity Credit Corporation
CIO   Committee for (later Congress of) Industrial Organization
CWA   Civil Works Administration
FDR   Franklin Delano Roosevelt
FERA   Federal Emergency Relief Administration
FSA   Farm Security Administration
NIRA   National Industrial Recovery Act
NRA   National Recovery Administration
PWA   Public Works Administration
RA   Resettlement Administration
REA   Rural Electrification Administration
RFC   Reconstruction Finance Corporation
TERA   Temporary Emergency Relief Administration
TNEC   Temporary National Economic Committee
TVA   Tennessee Valley Authority
WPA   Works Progress (later Projects) Administration

Chronology

The main acts and events of the New Deal are listed below in chronological order. Most of the acts are discussed in more detail in the text but, where appropriate, further information is given. There are limited references to events in other countries and to foreign policy initiatives in order to provide the necessary context. For the period after 1939, entries in the chronology are kept to a minimum and concentrate on domestic reform.

1928

6 November	FDR elected as Governor of New York.
	Herbert Hoover elected as President of the US.

1929

1 January	FDR inaugurated as Governor.
4 March	Hoover inaugurated as President.
15 June	Agricultural Marketing Act established Federal Farm Board.
24 October	'Black Thursday' on Wall Street.
29 October	'Black Tuesday' with 16.5 million shares sold on Wall Street.

1930

17 June	Smoot–Hawley Act imposed high tariffs on imports.
11 December	Failure of the Bank of the United States.

1931

11 May	Credit Anstalt (Austria's central bank) collapsed.
20 June	Moratorium (one year) on reparation and war debt payments.

17 August	President's Organization for Unemployment Relief formed.
18 September	New York state passed State Unemployment Relief Act.
21 September	UK abandoned gold standard.
September	Japan invaded Manchuria.
27 October	National Government elected in UK with an overwhelming Conservative majority.

1932

22 January	Congress authorized the Reconstruction Finance Corporation (RFC).
27 June–2 July	Democratic National Convention met in Chicago.
2 July	FDR made his famous 'New Deal' speech.
16 July	RFC authorized to lend $300 million to states for relief and given a further $1.5 billion for public works.
8 November	FDR elected as President of the US with 22.8 million votes to Hoover's 15.8 million.

1933

30 January	Adolf Hitler became Chancellor of Germany.
January–March	Worsening financial panic. By 4 March, thirty-four states had closed their banks. In nine others, tight restrictions were imposed.
4 March	FDR inaugurated as President.
5 March	FDR called a special session of Congress to meet on 9 March. He declared a four-day bank holiday.

THE FIRST HUNDRED DAYS

9 March	Emergency Banking Relief Act passed in a single day.
11 March	Economy Act.
12 March	The first 'fireside chat'.
22 March	Beer–Wine Revenue Act.
27 March	Farm Credit Administration created by executive order, to consolidate all federal agricultural credit agencies.

31 March	Civilian Conservation Corps (CCC) created.
6 April	The Black Bill (thirty-hour week) passed by Congress.
19 April	US taken off the gold standard.
12 May	Agricultural Adjustment Act.
	Federal Emergency Relief Administration authorized.
18 May	Tennessee Valley Act.
27 May	Federal Securities Act.
13 June	Home Owners Refinancing Act.
16 June	Banking Act.
	Farm Credit Act enabled Farm Credit Administration (FCA) to refinance farm mortgages.
	National Industrial Recovery Act (NIRA).
	Congress adjourned.

END OF FIRST HUNDRED DAYS

12 June–27 July	London Economic Conference.
5 July	FDR sent message which effectively sabotaged London Economic Conference.
14 July	Nazi Party declared to be the only legal political party in Germany.
October	Germany withdrew from the League of Nations.
8 November	Civil Works Administration (CWA) created. Ended March 1934.

1934	
January	Dr Francis Townsend set up Old Age Revolving Pension Scheme.
	Huey Long established the 'Share the Wealth' movement.
30 January	Gold Reserve Act reduced gold content of dollar.
31 January	Farm Mortgage Refinancing Act.
7 April	Jones–Connally Relief Act extended provisions of AAA to other commodities, for example barley, rye, cattle.
21 April	Bankhead Act (Cotton Control Act).

9 May	Jones–Costigan Sugar Act.
6 June	Securities Exchange Act created Securities and Exchange Commission.
12 June	Reciprocal Trade Agreements Act.
19 June	Silver Purchase Act.
28 June	National Housing Act established Federal Housing Administration.
	Taylor Grazing Act.
22 August	The American Liberty League formed.
30 August	Budget Director Lewis Douglas resigned over FDR's fiscal policies.
6 November	Congressional mid-term elections gave the Democratic party an increased majority.
11 November	Reverend Charles Coughlin formed the National Union for Social Justice.

1935

4 January	FDR's State of the Union message called for social reform.
8 April	Emergency Relief Appropriation Act ($5 billion).
27 April	Soil Conservation Act.
1 May	Resettlement Administration formed.
11 May	Rural Electrification Administration created.
27 May	In a 9–0 decision, the Supreme Court declared the National Recovery Administration (NRA) unconstitutional.

SECOND HUNDRED DAYS

19 June	FDR asked Congress for increased inheritance and income taxes.
26 June	National Youth Administration created.
5 July	National Labor Relations Act (Wagner Act).
14 August	Social Security Act.
22 August	Public Utility Holding Company Act.
23 August	Banking Act strengthened hand of Federal Reserve Board over regional banks.
30 August	Revenue Act, or Wealth Tax Act, increased taxes.
31 August	First Neutrality Act.

END OF SECOND HUNDRED DAYS

8 September	Huey Long assassinated.
9 November	Committee for Industrial Organization (CIO) formed.
23 December	FDR ordered the dissolution of NRA on 1 January 1936.

1936
6 January	The Supreme Court declared the AAA to be unconstitutional.
17 February	Tennessee Valley Authority (TVA) upheld by the Supreme Court.
29 February	Soil Conservation and Domestic Allotment Act.
7 March	German troops reoccupied the Rhineland.
May	Italy conquered Ethiopia.
1 June	The Supreme Court reaffirmed its denial to New York state of the right to fix minimum wages for women and children.
July	Spanish Civil War began.
3 November	FDR re-elected by a landslide, with 27.5 million votes to Landon's 16.7 million.

1937
6 January	FDR's annual message to Congress attacked the Judicial branch of government.
20 January	FDR's second Inaugural address stressed social reform.
5 February	FDR proposed a bill to reform the Supreme Court.
29 March	Supreme Court upheld Washington state minimum wage law.
12 April	Supreme Court upheld the National Labor Relations Act.
18 May	Justice Van Devanter announced his retirement from the Supreme Court.
24 May	Supreme Court upheld the Social Security Act.
22 July	Senate finally killed the 'court-packing' bill. Bankhead–Jones Farm Tenancy Act created Farm Security Administration.

July	Japan invaded mainland China.
August	Economy went into recession.
1 September	Wagner–Steagall National Housing Act established United States Housing Authority, with funds for slum clearance.
November	Special session of Congress called to deal with economic reform. Congress blocked all measures.

1938

3 January	In State of the Union Message, FDR promised a special monopoly message to Congress.
16 February	Second Agricultural Adjustment Act.
29 April	FDR asked Congress for an investigation of the concentration of economic power.
27 May	The Revenue Act of 1938 became law without the President's signature. It reduced taxes on large corporations.
16 June	Temporary National Economic Committee was set up to investigate monopolies.
24 June	Congress passed Food, Drug and Cosmetics Act.
25 June	Fair Labor Standards Act.
June	Congress voted $3.75 billion for public spending.
July	FDR launched purge of conservative Democrats.
29 September	Munich conference on the Czechoslovakia question.
8 November	Republicans made gains in Congressional elections.

1939

4 January	FDR's State of the Union message focused on foreign affairs.
16 March	German troops occupied Czechoslovakia.
3 April	Administrative Reorganization Act.
30 June	Emergency Relief Appropriation Act.
10 August	Amendment to the Social Security Act, extending the coverage, but postponing increased taxes.
3 September	UK and France declared war on Germany.

1940

12 June   German army entered Paris.

25 June   RFC authorized to finance construction of defence plants.

5 November   FDR re-elected by 27.2 million votes to Wilkie's 22.3 million.

1941

6 January   President's annual message referred to the Four Freedoms.

7 January   Office of Production Management created.

11 March   Lend-Lease Act.

11 April   Office of Price Administration created.

25 June   Fair Employment Practice Committee created.

15 August   Atlantic Charter signed.

7 December   Japanese planes attacked Pearl Harbor.

8 December   Congress declared war against Japan.

11 December   Germany declared war on the USA.

1942

12 January   War Labor Board created.

16 January   War Production Board created.

2 October   Anti-Inflation Act.

3 October   Office of Economic Stabilization created.

21 October   Revenue Act increased taxes.

3 November   Mid-term elections brought large gains to Republicans.

1943

22 February   Revenue bill vetoed by FDR, angered by amendments adopted by Congress which reduced income from taxation.

26 June   War Labor Disputes Act passed over FDR's veto.

1944

25 February   FDR's veto of 1944 Revenue Act overridden by Congress.

1–22 July   Bretton Woods Conference.

28 October   FDR made the Economic Bill of Rights speech.

7 November	FDR won fourth term with 25.6 million popular votes to Dewey's 22 million.
12 April	Death of FDR. Harry Truman became President.
8 May	VE Day.
14 August	VJ Day.
6 September	Truman called for a relaunch of New Deal reform in message to Congress.
8 October	Truman called for the Economic Bill of Rights.

CHAPTER I

Introduction

On 2 July 1932, Governor Franklin Delano Roosevelt (FDR) of New York state flew from Albany to Chicago, where the Democratic Party was holding its national convention. In an unprecedented move, FDR chose to accept in person his Party's nomination of him as its candidate for the 1932 Presidential election. Addressing the Convention delegates, he stated that 'I pledge you, I pledge myself, to a new deal for the American people'.[1] These words had been drafted by his close adviser and speechwriter, Samuel Rosenman, but the term 'New Deal' had not been used by Roosevelt before then. However, following the enthusiasm with which commentators and cartoonists seized upon the expression, it became the catch-phrase used then, and since, to describe the policies and programme adopted after FDR assumed the Presidency eight months later, on 4 March 1933.

President Roosevelt came to office at a time of national crisis. Over three years of economic depression had culminated in a series of banking panics which threatened the entire financial system. The New Deal order associated with his first two terms was a response to the severe world-wide depression which affected both industrial nations and primary producers in the early years of the 1930s. Debate continues as to the precise cause (or causes) of the Depression.[2] It is, however, beyond question that the United States, as a country which combined industrial superiority with a strong primary sector, was particularly badly affected, and, indeed, did not recover fully from the effects of the Depression until the Second World War. The American experience is often compared with that of France, Great Britain, and Germany, providing some useful parallels and contrasts.[3] The impact of the Depression was far greater in the United States than in Great Britain, where the south-east and the new industries enjoyed a boom during the later 1930s. Indeed, the United States experienced economic problems on a par with those facing the unstable government of Weimar Germany. However, there is a marked

I

contrast between the political consequences for the two countries. While
the United States retained a democratic system throughout the crisis, in
Germany, economic depression was accompanied by radical political
change. Thus, despite failing to solve its economic problems until the
onset of war, the American government succeeded in diverting potential
political difficulties. In seeking to understand this apparent paradox, an
important factor is the New Deal, its achievements and the grass-root
effects of its various programmes.

The New Deal lasted a comparatively short time. Commencing in
March 1933, the major legislative measures comprising the programme
were passed in the two 'Hundred Days' of 1933 and 1935, with a smaller
group of measures in 1937–8. Thereafter, the New Deal effectively
declined, although elements of the reform impulse may still be detected
in the War years. The main shape of the New Deal legislation was
fashioned by President Roosevelt, his cabinet colleagues (many of whom
remained in office throughout the New Deal; for example, Secretary of
Labor Frances Perkins and Secretary of the Interior Harold Ickes), more
informal advisers, such as Rexford Tugwell, Raymond Moley, Benjamin
Cohen and Thomas Corcoran, and the many lower-rank New Dealers
who staffed the burgeoning departments in Washington. President
Roosevelt resurrected the habit begun by his Democratic predecessor,
Woodrow Wilson, of sending to Congress carefully drafted measures
prepared by the executive, comprising a clear legislative programme.
Thus, while some of the acts passed had their origins in private bills
(notably the Wagner Act of 1935), for the most part the main legislative
achievements of the New Deal were the work of the Administration. The
consequence was a far-reaching programme of legislation which provided relief for millions of Americans, introduced a number of substantial
reforms and sought, albeit with only limited success, to achieve economic
recovery.

Commentators then, and historians since, have speculated and theo-
rized about the genesis, intentions and ultimate consequences of this New
Deal programme. Historical opinion has varied considerably. During the
1940s and 1950s, most historians were firmly within the liberal consensus
and saw the New Deal as being part of the same liberalism.[4] Debate
centred around where exactly to locate the New Deal within the progressive continuum. Was it, for example, a revolution, or did it represent
rather an evolution from a progressive heritage? If the latter, did it owe
its genesis to the New Nationalism of Theodore Roosevelt or to the New

Freedom of Woodrow Wilson? Should it be seen as the reawakening of policies and approaches articulated during the war effort of the First World War? Through their emphasis on the high politics of Washington DC, and a preoccupation with the antecedents of the New Deal, the liberal historians were less concerned with the consequences in the country. The New Left historians of the 1960s and 1970s soon remedied this partial omission. For writers such as Paul Conkin and Howard Zinn, the New Deal was remarkable, not so much for what it had achieved, as for the lost opportunities to attack the stranglehold of capitalism and address such fundamental social problems as civil rights and the appalling conditions faced by the sharecroppers of the South. Paul Conkin commented that 'the story of the New Deal is a sad story, the ever recurring story of what might have been'.[5] The very considerable political and constitutional limitations to such radical change, not to mention the lack of support for such a drastic programme among the American people, were rarely considered in detail.

Since the 1970s, studies of the New Deal have often moved beyond Washington DC to examine the consequences of the various programmes.[6] If such studies have demonstrated the often limited nature of such achievements, they have also made plain the very real constraints faced by those seeking to implement the New Deal at local level. While the New Deal may not have succeeded in remaking the American socio-economic structure, it did contain many administrators who were aware of the scope of the problem and who tried to the best of their ability to address it.

None the less, on the whole, recent historical interpretations of the New Deal have tended to emphasize its limitations as a reforming, radical force. Many of its achievements helped to institutionalize and consolidate the existing *status quo* in both economic and political spheres. Certainly, it saved capitalism, rejigged the existing socio-economic structure to remove some of the more glaring abuses and made concessions towards the most adversely affected groups of Americans. Conversely, it also reinforced the prevailing gender stereotypes, incorporated organized labour into a regulated contractual relationship with capital and failed to address critical issues such as the racial discrimination endemic in American society (particularly in the South). Many of its longest-lasting effects were virtually coincidental, most notably changes in the role of the federal government, the strengthening of the executive branch and the beginning of an 'imperial presidency'. However, at the time, the New

Deal succeeded in winning such strong support from ordinary Americans that it changed the nature of the Democratic Party permanently. This was partly due to the immense sense of achievement and change felt by many contemporaries, but it also reflects the significance of the intangible, subjective aspects of the New Deal, particularly its restoration of confidence among the public. It is in this vital area that one of Roosevelt's major contributions lies.

The New Deal is inextricably linked to Franklin Delano Roosevelt.[7] The 32nd President of the United States, he served for an unprecedented – and unequalled – twelve years in the Presidency. He was, in many ways, an untypical reformer and an unlikely presidential figure at a time of acute economic depression. Born in 1882, he came from the Hudson River gentry, had a privileged upbringing and never had to earn his own living, although at various times he pursued legal and business careers. His determined pursuit of a political career began in New York state politics before the First World War, led to the post of Assistant Secretary of the Navy in President Wilson's administration, and culminated in his nomination as the Democratic Party's vice-presidential candidate in 1920 (the Republican candidate, Warren Harding, won the election). However, his hopes of resuming his political activities were apparently dashed in 1921 when he suffered an attack of polio which left him effectively crippled. With determined effort, he could appear to walk, but only with callipers, crutches or the support of a strong arm. Given the contemporary attitude towards the disabled, it seemed likely that he would have to abandon any thought of a political career. However, his name remained prominent in Democratic politics throughout the 1920s, first because of his wife Eleanor, who played a major role in New York state Democratic party politics, then by his association with Al Smith, who urged him to run for State Governor in 1928. His record in the Governorship, and his astute lobbying and networking within the national Democratic Party, was sufficient to overcome his handicap, and in July 1932 he finally carried his party's nomination. His election as President in November 1932 launched the New Deal on the national stage.

However, the New Deal was not simply, nor even mainly, about one single man. To understand the evolution and implementation of its policies it is important to look beyond the White House, and indeed, beyond the close-knit circle in Washington DC, to the thousands of administrators who between them shaped the New Deal. The proliferation of agencies during the 1930s demanded an influx of new staff who helped shape the many programmes through their enthusiasm and beliefs. The New Deal was a remarkably informed programme. While the political aspects of Roosevelt's Presidency were entrusted to shrewd political operators with much experience of smoke-filled rooms – Louis Howe, James Farley and Edward Flynn, for example – the evolution of policies rested in different hands. For many of his cabinet appointees, Roosevelt drew upon social workers and progressive reformers. At the lower echelons, he looked to young, enthusiastic college graduates.

Moreover, outside the federal capital, the New Deal also relied upon a diverse group for its implementation. The 1930s revolutionized the role of federal government in American society, bringing every American into far more direct contact with the national government. This was clearly due to the legislation passed which impinged on the lives of so many, such as the recovery measures of the First Hundred Days, the numerous relief agencies, the Tennessee Valley Authority (TVA) and the Social Security Act. For many Americans, however, their experience of the New Deal was mediated, either by the complex network of federal-state arrangements created by a number of the New Deal acts, or by the day-to-day administration of the various programmes by the literally thousands of New Dealers. As individual administrators devised works projects, allocated relief, created Subsistence Homesteads, organized business codes, held National Labor Relations Board hearings and organized committees of farmers, they shaped the real New Deal experience for most Americans. The New Deal was not only about Roosevelt, Perkins, Ickes and Harry Hopkins devising schemes in Washington, it was the African American student put through college by the National Youth Administration's scholarships and work programmes, the teenage hobo given a place at a Civilian Conservation Corps (CCC) camp, the impoverished artist painting murals on the local post office and the unemployed constructing playgrounds for deprived children.

Thus, the New Deal was made not simply in Washington, but in towns, cities and states throughout the United States. With programmes accepted by Congress in which a large area of discretion was given to the President, the room for creative administration was considerable. However, the frequent emphasis upon local implementation and administration also opened the way for widespread discrimination and prejudice, whether on grounds of race, gender or behaviour. To understand not only the successes, but also the failings, of the New Deal, we have to go beyond the legislation and political manoeuvring in Washington to appreciate how it functioned. This is, perforce, a complex picture to convey; every locality, every agency, every relief scheme, had its own particular strengths and weaknesses, its own successes and failures. All, however, had their origins in the Depression experience which created the political will to implement far-reaching programmes of change and the popular support for those advocating action.

Notes

1. Speech to the Democratic convention, 2 July 1932, in S. I. Rosenman (ed.), *The Public Papers and Addresses of Franklin D. Roosevelt, 1928–1945* (13 vols, Random House: New York, 1938–50, hereafter *Roosevelt Papers*, plus volume), I, pp. 647–59.
2. Helpful discussions of the various explanations offered by historians may be found in Michael A. Bernstein, *The Great Depression: Delayed Recovery and Economic Change in America, 1929–1939* (Cambridge University Press: Cambridge, 1987) and C. P. Kindleberger, *The World in Depression 1929–1939* (Allen Lane: London, 1973).
3. Useful comparisons are made in Peter Temin, *Lessons from the Great Depression* (MIT Press: Cambridge, Mass., 1989) and John A. Garraty, 'A Comparative Approach: The New Deal, National Socialism, and the Great Depression', in Alonzo L. Hamby (ed.), *The New Deal: Analysis and Interpretation* (Longman: New York, 1981).
4. Two of the best-known liberal historians are William Leuchtenburg, *Franklin D. Roosevelt and the New Deal 1932–1940* (Harper and Row: New York, 1963) and Arthur Meier Schlesinger Jr, *The Age of Roosevelt* (3 vol, Heinemann: London, 1957–61).
5. Paul Conkin, *The New Deal* (Routledge: London, 1968), p. 73. See also Howard Zinn (ed.), *New Deal Thought* (Bobbs-Merrill: New York, 1966).
6. It is more difficult to point to classic examples of this approach. One possibility is Anthony J. Badger, *The New Deal: The Depression Years, 1933–1940* (Macmillan: London, 1989).
7. Biographies of FDR are listed in the Suggestions for Further Reading. My own views are expressed in a short study, Fiona Venn, *Franklin D. Roosevelt* (Cardinal: London, 1990).

CHAPTER 2

The Depression

Before exploring the initiation and implementation of the New Deal, it is important to understand something of the genesis and consequences of the massive slump which hit the American economy in the years between 1929 and 1933. The exact causes of the Depression are hotly debated, particularly between the monetarists and the Keynesians,[1] but whatever they were, the impact they had on the American economy was devastating. During the four-year period, Gross National Product fell by 30 per cent, industrial production virtually halved and farm prices fell by about 60 per cent. The construction industry was badly hit and investment fell dramatically. Unemployment rose from 3 per cent to around a quarter of the work-force. Few in the United States were prepared for such a disaster, for the 1920s had ostensibly been a decade of unparalleled prosperity. Business expansion had been accompanied by extremely rapid increases in productivity and output. Particularly striking was the rise in consumer durables, as the vast expansion in electricity supply had triggered a growth in ownership of refrigerators, irons, washing machines and radios. By 1929, over 16 million homes, accounting for over 60 per cent of the population, had electricity. Car ownership had soared, with over five million cars produced in 1929 alone. In the same year, there were 26 million registered automobiles. The move towards a mass consumption society, accompanied by large gains in productivity, stimulated the new mass production industries and had a positive economic effect. The 1920s trained many Americans to expect a high standard of living. Meanwhile, American firms consolidated and merged, with large corporations in a number of fields, exercising monopolistic or oligopolistic power. There were indeed strong grounds for optimism about the American economy during the 1920s. In the 1928 Presidential election, Herbert Hoover, soon to be elected President of the United States, suggested that 'We in America today are nearer to the final triumph over poverty than ever before in the history of any land. The poorhouse is vanishing from among us . . . we shall soon with the help of God be in sight of the day when poverty will be banished from the nation.'[2]

Along with the economic prosperity went political complacency and conservatism. The reform impulse which had characterized the late nineteenth and early twentieth centuries, known as the Progressive movement, disappeared. Republican incumbents occupied the White House from March 1921 until March 1933. They preached the value of minimum government interference in the economy, tax cuts, balanced budgets and low interest rates. As befitted the party of big business, the Secretary of the Treasury for much of the 1920s was millionaire Andrew Mellon, whose 1926 budget considerably reduced the tax paid by the wealthy. Herbert Hoover epitomized the era, first as Secretary of Commerce from March 1921, and then as President from March 1929. Originally from a poor background in rural Iowa, Hoover, through his own efforts, became a mining engineer and a millionaire. Meanwhile, the Democratic Party was preoccupied with internal divisions on questions such as prohibition, the standing of the Ku Klux Klan and the relative importance of the Party's rural and urban wings. Even without such divisions, however, it is doubtful whether the Democrats could have defeated the Republican Party in the 1928 election, for the Republicans were clearly associated with the booming economy and apparent prosperity.

However, this apparent prosperity was flawed. The new boom industries were unable to generate permanent growth. Increases in wages lagged behind those in profits and productivity, so that the workers, now also major consumers, lacked the additional capacity to sustain a high level of demand. While some more enlightened employers, especially in the capital-intensive new industries, recognized that their workers – and those of other companies – were also their consumers, most employers were not as farsighted.[3] During the 1920s, unions were in a state of decline, partly as a response to increased prosperity for workers, and partly because of the various policies pursued by employers, ranging from aggressive anti-unionism to more benevolent welfare capitalism and company 'unions' whose role was strictly circumscribed. Employees were therefore vulnerable to any downturn in demand. Moreover, in the days before built-in obsolescence, large purchases (often financed by credit) were seen as one-off transactions, with no expectation of frequent replacement. Thus, for example, in the automobile market a strong trade in second-hand cars developed, despite attempts to introduce new models and colours to attract customers. The mass production industries, therefore, were liable to experience a decline in demand in due course, although this was not recognized at the time.

The new prosperity did not include all Americans. Although workers in the new mass production industries earned high wages, they were also subject to seasonal lay-offs. Wages in the country remained very localized, with the South in particular relying upon its position as a low wage region to attract industry. The distribution of income became even more skewed during the 1920s. In 1929 the Brookings Institution published a survey entitled *America's Capacity to Consume* which pointed to the fact that the top 0.1 per cent of American families had an aggregate income equivalent to that of the bottom 42 per cent. Moreover, that same small group of families held a third of all savings; two-thirds of total savings were held by less than 3 per cent of families. Yet, at the same time, government figures suggested that well over half the country's households earned less than the sum defined by the Bureau of Labor as a 'decent standard of living'.[4] There were other fundamental weaknesses detectable with hindsight, if not to most contemporaries. The agricultural sector, still critical within the overall American economy, had been weak since the early 1920s, as a glut of primary commodities on the world market caused prices to collapse. From an index of 217 in 1919 (based on 1910–14 as 100) prices had fallen to 148 in 1929.[5] This again reduced the pool of customers for the mass production industries. Moreover, the weakness of the rural economy had other implications for the United States as a whole. Having overexpanded in the 'golden age' caused by the First World War, many farmers found themselves in serious debt. Total farm mortgages in the United States rose from $6,700 million in 1920 to $9,400 million in 1925. This placed considerable strain upon the rural banking sector, which contained many of the smaller and more vulnerable banks in a system itself prone to difficulties. The Federal Reserve System did not cover all the nation's banks by any means, and was limited in how far it could control even those under its jurisdiction. Thus, the banking sector was easily affected by over-extended credit policies.

Moreover, the international economy was also dislocated by the War. The United States had emerged from the First World War as the world's leading economic power, but unlike Great Britain in the years up to 1913, it did not pursue policies that would stabilize the world economy. Instead, by its stand on war debts and tariffs, coupled with massive gains in productivity and virtual self-sufficiency, the United States exacerbated gold imbalances and economic nationalism. Successive American governments ignored calls from their co-belligerents in the First World War to reduce or overturn the debts which the Allied governments had incurred with the Government of the United States, while simultaneously making it difficult for those countries to earn dollars with which to repay the loans by a combination of high tariffs and its own economic boom. Moreover, the imbalance between the United States and the rest of the world was exacerbated as American citizens themselves invested abroad.

These flaws had, of course, existed during the 1920s but at that time were hidden from view. It was the Wall Street Crash, which dramatically signalled the weaknesses in the American boom, together with the subsequent international banking crises and the further spiral into depression which allowed these flaws to emerge into the open. For at least two years, from 1927 to 1929, the American stock market had been gripped by speculative fever. The New York Times Industrial Index, which at the end of 1927 stood at 245, had increased to 331 by the end of the following year, and by September 1929 stood at 452. In such a speculative market, where many shares were bought on margin (that is, on credit), there was a strong possibility of over-extension and collapse. Once prices started going down heavily, as they did on Black Thursday (24 October 1929), followed by the even blacker Black Tuesday (29 October 1929), speculators rushed to sell their own shares and the resultant panic pushed down prices with great rapidity. On 29 October, over 16 million shares changed hands and the index fell 45 points in one day.[6] Thus, the Wall Street Crash apparently marked the break between the prosperity decade and the depression decade. In itself, a stock market crisis need not have greatly affected the overall economic performance. Only a small proportion of the population invested on the stock market and not all of them lost more than they could readily afford.[7] However, in a country which had come to expect the permanence of prosperity, the psychological impact of the stock market decline was significant. Moreover, it hit particularly hard at the provision of credit, for many credit institutions, including the poorly regulated banking sector, had invested a lot of money in the stock market, and were thus adversely affected when it collapsed. None the less, there were underlying signs of economic difficulties even before the Crash. Industrial indices were beginning to move downwards as early as July 1929, a trend exacerbated by the loss in confidence. In the summer of 1929, new car sales and building construction, two important indices of consumer activity, had declined.

Meanwhile, the impact of the American stock market boom, and its subsequent decline, upon credit in Europe was considerable. American investors in Europe had not always lent wisely, putting strain on the international credit structure. In the stock market boom, many Americans had removed funds from Europe to place them on Wall Street instead. As the free flow of capital began to diminish, vulnerable economies, Germany, for example, found it difficult to cope, while the results of the Wall Street Crash led many investors to abandon risky investments. As a consequence, pressure grew upon any weak currency, particularly following the collapse of Austria's largest bank, the Credit-Anstalt, in the early summer of 1931. Hungary, Germany and ultimately Great Britain abandoned the gold standard in subsequent months. In the United States, a growing domestic bank crisis after August 1931 meant that by January 1932 over 1,800 banks had failed. Even before this, in view of the uncertain economic climate, the problems with credit and a decline in confidence, American businessmen began to reduce stocks and production, laying off workers as a consequence. This had repercussions, not only within the domestic economy, but also on foreign markets from which the Americans purchased. It also caused dramatic increases in unemployment, from under 500,000 in October 1929 to over four million in January 1930, and approximately eight million in 1931. By January 1933, the numbers unemployed had reached somewhere between 13 million and 17 million – a quarter to a third of the work-force.[8] Others, still in work, faced savage reductions in hours and wages. Farm prices plummeted, falling below not only the cost of production, but, in many instances, the cost of transportation to market. While goods rotted in the fields, in the cities the unemployed destitute starved. For many farmers, economic decline brought personal tragedy, as almost one million farms were repossessed between 1930 and 1934. The United States, then, faced a crisis which encompassed not only the financial, but also the industrial and agricultural, spheres.

The decline into depression was not, it must be stressed, immediate and complete. There were periods of apparent partial recovery, with rallies in economic performance. To some extent, this allowed a false sense of confidence, a belief that this depression could be tackled, as all previous depressions had been, by a combination of market forces and exhortation. No tradition existed in the United States of federal government intervention in the workings of the economy at times of weakness. However, even if the economy were to right itself in time, the extent of human suffering demanded attention. In addition to those out of work, there were the long-term poor, the old, the sick, single parent families and the rural Southern population. The bank crises which hit in the years 1931–33 wiped out the savings of literally millions of Americans. Agricultural distress had existed even within the prosperous 1920s and was, of course, greatly exacerbated by the Depression.

However, this was a world-wide phenomenon. Germany, for example, suffered a drop in industrial production similar to that of the United States, while in Great Britain unemployment increased from around 10 per cent of the insured work-force to over 20 per cent. The British Exchequer experienced increased costs because of the provision of unemployment insurance, both of the insured payments and also the payments made to those within the insurance system who had not met all of the required criteria – the so-called dole. In 1929 expenditure on unemployment relief was £47 million, in 1931 it was £92 million; but, with a welfare safety net in place, the British government did not face the same crisis of public confidence in the government as that faced by Hoover. Although the Labour Government headed by Ramsay MacDonald collapsed, occasioned by a severe split in the Cabinet on the issue of whether to cut unemployment benefit, MacDonald himself, and his conservatively inclined Chancellor of the Exchequer, Philip Snowden, remained in office, in a coalition National Government.[9]

The situation in Germany was far closer to that of the United States. The German economy had already experienced a period of instability and inflation in the period 1923–24, and its subsequent stability owed much to American loans, hence it was vulnerable to any withdrawal of capital or confidence. During the speculative fever which gripped the United States during 1928–29, and its subsequent collapse, there was a substantial outflow of American capital. Germany was already experiencing a depression by the summer of 1929. Economic crisis encouraged businessmen in the heavy industry sector to increase their calls for tax cuts and a decrease in the welfare provision of the Constitution. In 1930 the Brüning government resorted to cuts in expenditure and tax reductions, but this simply led to increased numbers of unemployed, while also having an adverse effect upon the lower middle classes. This created a fertile ground for the strategies of Adolf Hitler and the Nazi party. The weakness of the Weimar Republic was further emphasized when Brüning was forced to resort to the device of emergency decrees signed by President Hindenburg in order to force through his stringent austerity package. When the Reichstag protested, it was promptly dissolved and Brüning thenceforth governed by his use of the President's emergency powers until May 1932. These policies simply undermined the credibility of democratic government and its abilities to meet the economic crisis which saw industrial production virtually halved in the three years from 1929 to 1932, while unemployment soared from under 1.5 million to over five million. Imports and exports were halved in value and pressure grew upon the German government to cut the welfare benefits available for the unemployed.[10]

However, it was small consolation for Americans to know that other countries were also affected by the Depression, for the domestic impact was severe. The economic downturn hit a country poorly prepared to meet the demands of mass unemployment. The United States in 1929 was a nation whose rural roots still dominated social values and political life. Not until 1920 did a majority of its population live in settlements of more than 2,500 and even then the attitudes and prejudices of small town living prevailed. The minds of Americans were still geared to the presumptions of close communities where it was assumed that the needy could rely on philanthropy and neighbourliness. Although this was no longer the case (if, indeed, it ever had been), Americans were unprepared to reject the reliance on voluntarism. At a time when other industrial powers had already established unemployment insurance, old age pensions and other welfare measures, the United States had only a very patchy and limited welfare provision, a position exacerbated by the prevailing federal system which generally left such issues to the individual states. The one major federal experiment in the provision of social welfare, the granting of pensions to Civil War veterans, had had a detrimental effect. The political corruption associated with these pensions militated against the adoption of universal benefits; instead, reformers turned their attention to the protection of women and children. As Theda Skocpol notes, welfare legislation prior to the New Deal concentrated on 'protecting soldiers and mothers'.[11] Even such basics as elementary factory legislation were still a matter of debate in the United States – it took until the 1930s to eradicate child labour. Unions represented only a small minority of the work-force and tended to concentrate upon bread and butter matters relating solely to the interests of their members, who were often the skilled élite of the work-force. There was no universal provision for the most vulnerable groups in society. Relief for the destitute was in many instances still provided in workhouses, and in some communities paupers were denied the vote. With no universal provision for those in need, other than local poor relief schemes which were hopelessly under-funded, the sudden mass destitution could not be adequately addressed.[12]

This situation should be compared with that of the two other leading industrial powers. In Great Britain, an extensive social security safety net was in place even before the First World War, and this had been strengthened thereafter. The 1897 Workmen's Compensation Act covered most workers by 1906, and in 1908 the Old Age Pensions Act had introduced non-contributory payments to people over 69. The 1911 National Insurance Act had introduced health insurance provisions which provided sickness benefit and free medical treatment to about 70 per cent of the population, and had also introduced unemployment insurance for some workers. Coverage of unemployment insurance was extended after the First World War, although it excluded agricultural workers (in 1931 the agricultural work-force comprised less than 10 per cent of the work-force). Dependants' allowances and widows' and orphans' pensions were also introduced, and from 1928 the old age pension was turned into a contributory scheme. These insurance benefits, which escaped the stigma of poor relief, were funded by contributions from the employer, the employee and the state. Thus, the British Gov-ernment had recognized that in a heavily industrialized economy, an individual could not provide for all the possible threats to one's livelihood. Germany, too, had moved towards the provision of a welfare programme. Under the guidance of Bismarck, it had put into place as early as the 1880s a programme of social insurance, as well as workmen's compensation, and by the time of the First World War also had in place a contributory old age insurance scheme.

The reasons for this discrepancy between the United States and the rest of the industrialized world were many and varied. The most intang-ible was the traditional emphasis within the United States of what Hoover described as 'rugged individualism', a sense that the country was a land of opportunity and that unemployment and destitution were the fault of the individual, not of society. The legacy of the frontier, of self-advancement through geographical mobility, was widespread, even if it never had the efficacy with which it was associated, and certainly not now in an era of mass industrialization. Moreover, reform groups, even when concerned with the problems of industrial cities, had not seen the answer as lying in universal welfare provision. One possible reason for this is that, whereas the reformers were generally middle-class WASPs (White Anglo-Saxon

Protestants), in the early twentieth century major American cities held large populations of immigrants and their children. In many cities, first- and second-generation immigrants made up the majority of the population, thus lending credence to the assumption that the city was an alien place. Moreover, the early incorporation of the lower classes into the voting population in the United States had lessened the pressure for organized working-class participation in the political process. The Socialist Party of the United States was far weaker than its German or British counterparts.

However, if there were cultural values and social divisions dictating the nature of the response, there were also structural reasons for the United States' limited response to the Depression when it came. A major reason for the lack of universal welfare provision was that matters of social policy were seen as the responsibility of the individual state governments and not of the federal government. Although some states did pass enlightened legislation and made provision for unemployment and old age, they were too few in number. As late as 1935, only one state, Wisconsin, had an unemployment insurance scheme, and only 28 states provided old age pensions in any form. The potential loss of businesses to a neighbouring state with less expensive restrictions on working practices prevented many states from providing for welfare, while Southern states, relying heavily on cheap labour for their attraction to industry, were unwilling to add further to the costs of employers. Other reasons explain the devastating impact of the Depression. The United States did not have a central bank accustomed to assuming an important role in the direction of the economy. The Federal Reserve System was only recent and only covered those banks which were registered under federal law. Overall the banking sector was weak, with too many small banks, highly localized in their clientele and resources, vulnerable to sudden downturns in the economy or to a run on their reserves. Moreover, the economy was still heavily reliant upon the agricultural sector, which had been in decline throughout the 1920s, the one area of the economy which did not join in the prosperity of that decade. Not only did that leave the rural banking sector vulnerable to depression, it also meant that suppressed demand in the rural economy was, even in the 1920s, a drag on prosperity.

The impact of the depression was, consequently, immense.[13] Manual workers had been used to providing for occasional periods of unemployment, without having to accept the ultimate humiliation of asking for official relief. Numerous expedients were adopted to avoid this;

possessions were pawned or sold, insurance policies surrendered, families moved in together to reduce rent. Many took to the road, the traditional response of mobile Americans to hard times and by 1932, instead of rural migration into towns and cities, there was a net outflow from the town to the countryside. Ultimately, however, as unemployment rates mounted, more and more Americans were forced to apply for relief, often to find that their local communities had exhausted their meagre funds. All accounts of the popular experience of the Depression stress the arbitrary nature of relief, depending upon where the applicant lived, when he applied for relief, even his family's moral standing and cleanliness. The sums (or food orders) provided differed widely in amount. For some, there was literally no relief available. Reports abounded of families forced to live in caves, garages and jerry-built shanties (the Hoovervilles of popular parlance). The destitute scavenged in rubbish heaps for food, or begged from house to house. Even for those on relief, it often provided only the barest of food necessities, with no provision for rent, clothing, or even the wherewithal to achieve a basic level of cleanliness. Daily, conditions in the worst hit areas negated the view held by President Hoover, and no doubt many other Americans too, that neighbourliness and community support would prevent starvation and destitution. Economic historians have pointed to infant mortality and death rate figures to argue that the impact of the Depression was not as catastrophic as some have suggested, but whatever the truth statistically, the fact none the less remains that the conditions existing on a wide scale in the United States were totally unacceptable in a modern, industrial, recently prosperous country.[14]

Thus, President Hoover faced, not the eradication of poverty, but economic crisis and personal suffering on a large scale. The question therefore arose as to the most appropriate policy for him to adopt. In many respects, Hoover must have seemed ideally suited for the role in which he found himself – a President having to deal with widespread need. He had a reputation as a remarkable administrator and a major humanitarian. Having made a fortune as a mining engineer within a very short time, he had been free to offer his services to the Wilson administration during the First World War. As United States Food Administrator, his name was synonymous with the relief efforts directed to war-ravaged Belgium. However, Hoover also had a very clear individual philosophy which he had further developed during his years as Secretary of Commerce. A self-made man himself, he believed strongly in the importance of individual effort, co-ordinated through voluntary groups if need be, and careful planning. His work in Europe in the aftermath of the First World War had been on these lines – trying to exhort his fellow Americans to aid the needy of Europe, but by voluntary meatless days and similar sacrifices, not by government direction.

It was through the route of voluntarism that Hoover tried to reconcile his humanitarian background with the economic orthodoxy at the time which dictated that he should seek to balance the budget, and also the tradition of the Republican administrations of the 1920s which had tended to distance the federal government from the management of the economy. As a successful businessman himself, he realized the importance of avoiding a vicious downward spiral as employers cut wages and hours, thus helping to reduce yet further the demand for their products. This was particularly important in a mass production, mass consumption economy. However, his initial response was one of exhortation and voluntarism, an attempt to invoke private initiative. Within a month of the Wall Street Crash he had obtained pledges from business leaders that they would maintain production and wage levels, while union leaders also agreed to co-operate in maintaining industrial peace. At the same time, he urged local and state governments to maintain their programmes of public works, or even to extend them. As a programme, this had much to recommend it. Whatever the promises, however, within a year there were clear cuts in production, employment and wage levels. In the face of continued depression, Hoover slowly expanded his administration's response to the economic crisis. Indeed, some historians have seen in him the precursor of the New Deal, a man who had tried, through his advocacy of a corporatist type policy based upon trade associations in the 1920s, to modernize the American economy, and who also sought, within the limits of his economic philosophy, to tackle the Depression.[15] Thus, Hoover advanced public works schemes and extended credit, most notably in 1932 through the Reconstruction Finance Corporation (RFC). However, this came more than two years into the Depression, by which time the crisis in the economy was clearly apparent.

In one important sector, however, the Hoover administration acted very promptly. The need for agricultural action had been recognized even before the Crash. In April 1929 Hoover called Congress into special session to address the pressing problems of the farmers. This led to more tariff protection and, in June 1929, as a result of the Agricultural Marketing Act, the establishment of a Federal Farm Board, although the latter's power relied mainly on the voluntary co-operation of farmers. The Board could encourage co-operatives, by loans if necessary (from $500 million appropriated for the purpose), and could also create stabilization corporations to purchase surplus crops, thus, it was hoped, maintaining agricultural prices. Initially, assistance was concentrated upon the most seriously affected agricultural commodities, grain and cotton, through the Cotton Stabilization Corporation and the Grain Stabilization Corporation. This was not enough to solve the major structural problems of agriculture, however, as it neither reduced production nor stimulated consumption. It became apparent that such schemes would only work if output was controlled and the experiment in price support was abandoned as massive surpluses built up. Attempts to protect the domestic market against imports was no more successful; not only did the United States import very little basic agricultural produce, but the 1930 Smoot–Hawley tariff was extended by Congressional pressure to cover industrial as well as agricultural commodities, thus increasing agricultural costs. Moreover, this tariff invited retaliation from other nations, and reduced still further the United States' foreign trade.

Nor did Hoover's policies towards other sectors of the economy prove any more effective. His administration engaged only in public spending which had already been budgeted, while his exhortations to businessmen to advance capital spending, for example on construction, had little effect. He recognized that one problem was the unavailability of credit, and in January 1932 set up the Reconstruction Finance Corporation under Charles Dawes and then Jesse Jones to assist with the provision of credit through large institutions such as banks. Jesse Jones was to remain in his position as head of the RFC until 1939, and it continued to play a significant role in the New Deal. However, in this early period, the extension of credit was not particularly significant as individual businesses were too worried by long-term business prospects even to wish to borrow. Moreover, the terms on which the RFC operated were carefully defined. It was given up to two billion dollars to rescue major institutions such as banks, big businesses and mortgage, loan and insurance companies, but many of its resources went to its largest clients. In the first two years of operation, about 7 per cent of its borrowers accounted for over half of the total sum lent. These loans were initially aimed at restoring confidence in the economy as a whole, rather than meeting the needs of the most vulnerable groups within it. Given Hoover's belief that the Depression was essentially a foreign phenomenon, and that the

American economy was fundamentally sound, it was unlikely that he would depart from his own principles and massively extend the boundaries of the federal government's responsibilities. Nor would he give money to assist states with the awesome task of providing for the unemployed, although in July 1932 he agreed that the RFC should be permitted to lend money for that purpose to those states which had exhausted their resources. However, to qualify, the state governments had to declare that they had reached the end of any constitutional means of securing funds, that is, borrowing and taxation. For most states therefore, RFC funding could only be used for self-financing projects which would generate sufficient revenue to pay back the loan. The only other gesture towards the destitute was the creation of the President's Emergency Committee for Employment, later renamed the President's Organization of Unemployment Relief, but this simply sought to persuade philanthropists and businessmen to increase voluntary donations. One further gesture towards helping ordinary Americans was the Federal Home Loan Bank Act, which set up home loan banks with capital of $125 million to enable finance companies to obtain funds without foreclosing on home owners. However, although a step in the right direction, it could lend no more than 50 per cent of the value of a property and thus did not really help most of those threatened with the loss of their homes.

It should be stressed that the normal practice in depressions was for the federal government to follow a policy of inaction, and thus Hoover went much further than any other previous President faced by economic crisis. However, as the Depression continued, so too did the burden of relief faced by the states. During the winter of 1931–32, first private charities, and then local and state governments, in the worst-hit regions of the United States found their funds exhausted. Unemployment tended to be highly concentrated, while the state governments most affected by the need to provide relief often also saw their income drop dramatically as the industries in the area laid off workers, and the income from sales taxes plummeted. Many state governments were also forbidden to borrow by their constitutions. The unprecedented nature of the problem was recognized by those responsible for administering local relief, and by the winter of 1931–32 leaders of charities, for example, Horatio Gates Lloyd who chaired Philadelphia's Committee for Unemployment Relief, and public officials such as Mayor Frank Murphy of Detroit, were calling for federal relief.[16]

Throughout the prosperous 1920s, the Republicans had appeared the natural party of government. However, in the face of Depression, and the worsening conditions, it seemed impossible for the Party to win the Presidential election which would take place in November 1932. As a consequence, there was considerable competition for the Democratic nomination. One of the strongest contenders was Al Smith, a previous governor of New York state, and the 1928 presidential nominee. As a Catholic Irish American, Smith had a strong appeal to the immigrants in the Northern industrial cities, but his strong anti-Prohibition ideas and assertive ethnic identity alienated potential Democratic voters in other parts of the country, notably the conservative, rural voters of the South and West. This had been clearly demonstrated in the 1928 election, in which Hoover had won a number of states in the previously 'solid' Democratic South, including North Carolina, Tennessee, Kentucky and Texas. In an electoral system which measured victory by state, Smith's major achievement in capturing the Northern industrial cities for his party was not immediately apparent. Hence, while many in the Party felt that Smith still had a strong claim on the nomination, others believed that he would prove a liability in a year which should see a Democratic victory, not only at Presidential level but in the Houses of Congress and state and local elections.

Of the other candidates, one of the most popular was Smith's successor as Governor of New York, Franklin D. Roosevelt. Elected in 1928, Roosevelt was therefore in office at the time of the Depression, and under his leadership the state had adopted one of the most far-reaching and innovative programmes ever seen at state level. Despite his own commitment to balanced budgets, he had undertaken deficit-financed relief operations, such as the Temporary Emergency Relief Administration (TERA), (created in October 1931) effectively run by Harry Hopkins, which provided funds for the unemployed. TERA had an initial appropriation of $20 million, financed through a sharp increase in state income tax and by January 1933 had distributed some $83 million in direct and work relief. At the same time, Roosevelt encouraged the exploration of wider issues, such as old age security, and tried to find ways of tackling the difficulty of providing national welfare coverage when such issues had traditionally been regarded as the responsibility of individual states. He took the initiative in pursuing national action through co-ordination with other state governors. He also advocated state-controlled unemployment insurance, financed by employers, employees and the state government. During this period, FDR was evolving his own political philosophy towards the Depression and an appropriate government response. It is best summed up in a message which he sent to the New York legislature in August 1931, which, while referring to the New York state legislature, had resonances at national level too.

> The duty of the State towards the citizens is the duty of the servant to the master . . . One of these duties of the State is that of caring for those of its citizens who find themselves the victims of such adverse circumstances as makes them unable to obtain even the necessities for mere existence without the aid of others . . .[17]

Governor Roosevelt had won the gubernatorial election by the narrowest margin in 1928, but he was easily re-elected in 1930, winning support from even traditional Republicans such as the farmers of the northern part of the state through his farm relief programme. Once re-elected, he could present himself as a potential candidate for the Democratic presidential nomination in 1932. However, he did not face an easy task, not only because of Smith's rivalry, but also because of his own background and history. Although the clear choice of the majority of the delegates at the 1932 Democratic Party convention, FDR faced a tough battle to secure the final nomination. As part of the negotiations at the convention, he accepted a conservative Southerner, John Nance Garner, as his running mate. Once successfully nominated, however, his eventual victory over the discredited Hoover was virtually inevitable.

As a consequence of the long drawn out American electoral system, FDR spent much of 1932 campaigning, and thus made a number of speeches setting out his principles and projected policies. In order to write these speeches, and assemble ideas for his future administration, he employed the talents of a number of academics and experts, known collectively as the 'Brain Trust'. The Brain Trust, with its emphasis upon policy, was entirely different (and distant) from the candidate's political team, comprising Louis Howe, James Farley and Edward Flynn. Set up at the instigation of one of his major speechwriters, Sam Rosenman, the Brain Trust included Raymond Moley, Rexford Tugwell and Adolf Berle, all professors at Columbia University.[18] All three were advocates of government-business co-operation and central planning of the economy, although, whereas Moley saw businessmen as playing the main role, Tugwell preferred the state to dominate. Berle, who with Gardiner Means had written an influential book on *The Modern Corporation and Private Property*, held a position midway between the other two.

The members of the Brain Trust presented a number of alternative stratagems to Roosevelt, helped him explore the diverse solutions offered to the country's crisis, and on many occasions wrote powerful and significant speeches. It was believed on the whole that the Depression's causes were domestic, that government needed to stimulate and control the economy, and that it should reject the Brandeisian emphasis upon the restoration of competition. Moley described this approach scornfully as the belief that 'If America could once more become a nation of small proprietors, of corner grocers and smithies under spreading chestnut trees, we should have solved the problems of American life'.[19]

One cannot see in the campaign speeches a complete foreshadowing of the New Deal, not least because many of the speeches were inherently contradictory and were, in any event, designed primarily to win votes, not to present a complete programme. However, in several of the speeches, a number of key ideas emerged: that in an industrial economy the presence of big business should be countered by the creation of a more powerful government; that efficient, national planning of the economy was necessary; that the problem of agricultural overproduction had to be tackled, not least because of its knock-on effect on the industrial economy; and that the federal government could not afford to ignore the ordinary individual citizen, the man described by Roosevelt as 'the forgotten man at the bottom of the economic pyramid'.[20] Many of his speeches foreshadowed the later emphasis upon under-consumption as the key to understanding the Depression. However, at the same time, Roosevelt was advocating a balanced budget and rating Hoover for his extravagance, while the Democratic platform had called for a balanced budget and economies in government spending. Nor did the rest of the party platform offer much guidance to the possible policies of a future Roosevelt administration. Its other main planks were a commitment to the repeal of Prohibition, government withdrawal from private enterprise, a sound currency and banking reform, lower tariffs, control of crop surpluses and the introduction of unemployment and old age insurance by the various state governments. In short, no one could be confident about the policies likely to be adopted by the Roosevelt administration.

Despite – or perhaps because of – this ambiguity, Franklin Roosevelt won the expected victory in November 1932, with a majority of 472 votes in the electoral college to Hoover's 59. The scale of the popular victory was less dramatic, but it was an undoubted rejection of Hoover and a clear mandate for Roosevelt, if not for any clear policy. However, the pattern of support for Roosevelt did not as yet demonstrate the emergence of a new Democratic coalition which was in the process of formation, but which was to consolidate and crystallize over the next four years. Indeed, Roosevelt's main strength appeared to be in the rural South and West, rather than Smith's industrial heartlands. These he certainly carried, but it was the winning over of the farmers of the West and the recapture of the solid South which guaranteed his victory. His political debts, therefore, in so far as he had any, were to the rural rather than the urban regions of the United States. The Socialist and Communist party candidates each polled less than a million votes, the latter only just over 100,000. Indications were, therefore, that the American electorate had rejected extreme responses to the economic crisis in the country and looked instead to the traditional two-party system to alleviate the depression. This is in marked contrast to the situation in Germany, where successive elections demonstrated an increased polarization of opinion between the extremes of Right and Left.

No one in November 1932 could easily have forecast the overall shape of the Roosevelt administration's likely plans for economic recovery. This was to prove significant in the four months' interregnum between the November election and Roosevelt's inauguration in March 1933.[21] During this time, uncertainty as to the policies likely to be followed by the new President, growing disillusion and mistrust of American financial institutions, and worsening conditions in the international economy all contributed to a worsening of the situation. Hoover continued to believe that the Depression was a foreign phenomenon, imported to the United States, and that it could therefore only be tackled at international level. Moreover, as a lame duck president, there was little that he could do to halt the steady deterioration of economic and social conditions. Many European governments were eager to take international action to address such fundamental issues as exchange rates, the gold standard, tariff levels and the intertwined issues of reparations and war debts, but Hoover felt unable to act decisively. Attempts were made by the outgoing administration to involve the President-elect in policy formation, but Hoover essentially sought to persuade Roosevelt to accept and approve his policies, on the grounds that this would restore confidence. Since such policies included a balanced budget, cuts in government spending and the rigid adherence to the exchange rate and gold standard, Roosevelt adamantly refused to tie his hands so categorically in advance. In this worsening situation, foreign investors exchanged their dollars for gold, and governors of a growing number of states took action to close or restrict their banking system, in an attempt to stall the rising tide of bank failures.[22]

By the time of the inauguration, the governors of 34 states had closed their states' banks, leaving millions of Americans facing the prospect of coping without access to money. More fundamental, if intangible, was the loss of morale, of confidence within the country at the time. Many, particularly among the wealthiest groups in society, feared that revolution might well break out among the desperate groups of the unemployed. Historians such as Piven and Cloward have emphasized the rise of spontaneous, radical action among the unemployed as Unemployed Councils and Unemployed Leagues sought to harness the instinctive anger of those who felt betrayed by their own society.[23] Others at the time noted the sense of apathy, the desire for strong leadership, which marked many Americans, a sense which some compared to the atmosphere in Fascist Italy. The Roosevelt administration faced a society which had lost faith in many of its own institutions, which had had the pillars of its beliefs shaken, and where many argued that the days of capitalism were numbered. Roosevelt had declared during the election campaign that 'The country needs and, unless I mistake its temper, the country demands bold, persistent experimentation'.[24] Within the first three months of taking office he was to provide it, in ample measure.

Notes

1. Compare Milton Friedman and Anna Jacobson Schwartz, *A Monetary History of the United States, 1867–1960* (Princeton University Press: Princeton, 1963) with Peter Temin, *Did Monetary Forces Cause the Great Depression?* (Norton: New York, 1976).
2. Herbert Hoover, quoted in Peter Fearon, *War, Prosperity and Depression: The U.S. Economy 1917–45* (Philip Allen: Oxford, 1987).
3. Colin Gordon, *New Deals: Business, Labor and Politics in America, 1920–1935* (Cambridge University Press: New York, 1994), pp. 35–165.
4. See Robert S. McElvaine, *The Great Depression: America 1929–41* (Times Books: New York, 1984), pp. 38–42.
5. Jim Potter, *The American Economy Between the World Wars* (Macmillan: London, 1985), p. 60.
6. For a perceptive and readable explanation and account of the Great Crash, see J. K. Galbraith, *The Great Crash 1929* (Penguin: London, 1977).
7. It is impossible to give a clear picture of the numbers involved in the stock market as no precise figures exist and historians themselves differ. Less than two million had invested enough to warrant the use of a broker.
8. Precise figures are also unavailable for the numbers unemployed as the federal government did not collect such statistics. Again, therefore, historians' estimates differ.

9. This brief account is based on Peter Dewey, *War and Progress: Britain 1914–1945* (Longman: Harlow, 1997).

10. See V. R. Berghahn, *Modern Germany: Society, economy and politics in the twentieth century* (Cambridge University Press: Cambridge, 1982).

11. Theda Skocpol, *Protecting Soldiers and Mothers: The Political Origins of Social Policy in the United States* (Harvard University Press: Cambridge, Mass., 1992).

12. William R. Brock, *Welfare, Democracy and the New Deal* (Cambridge University Press: Cambridge, 1988). See also James T. Patterson, *America's Struggle Against Poverty: 1900–1980* (Harvard University Press: Cambridge, Mass., 1981).

13. For a graphic description of the effect of the Depression, see Studs Terkel, *Hard Times: An Oral History of the Great Depression* (Pantheon Books: New York, 1970).

14. On mortality rates, see Potter, *The American Economy*, pp. 31–2.

15. Ellis W. Hawley, 'Herbert Hoover, the Commerce secretariat and the vision of an "Associative State" 1921–28', *Journal of American History* 41 (1974), pp. 116–40, explores Hoover's views in the 1920s. For a discussion of Hoover's response to the Depression, see Albert U. Romasco, *The Poverty of Abundance: Hoover, the Nation and the Depression* (Oxford University Press: New York, 1965).

16. Bonnie Fox Schwartz, *The Civil Works Administration, 1933–1934: The Business of Emergency Employment in the New Deal* (Princeton University Press: Princeton, 1984), pp. 15–21.

17. Message to the Legislature, 28 August 1931, quoted in Samuel I. Rosenman, *Working with Roosevelt* (Rupert Hart-Davis: London, 1952), p. 59. For a detailed study of the Roosevelt Governorship, see Kenneth S. Davis, *FDR: The New York Years 1928–1933* (Random House: New York, 1985).

18. There is a difference of opinion as to whether this select group should be referred to as the Brain Trust or the Brains Trust. In their memoirs (listed in Suggestions for Further Reading), Moley and Tugwell refer to the Brains Trust, while Rosenman prefers Brain Trust.

19. Raymond Moley, *After Seven Years* (Harper and Brothers: New York, 1939), p.24.

20. Rosenman, *Roosevelt Papers*, I, pp. 624–7.

21. This was the last time that the interregnum lasted four months. By the Twentieth Amendment to the Constitution, which had already been passed and came into force in February 1933, from 1937 the new Administration took office in January following a November election.

22. For an account of Hoover's attempts to secure a joint statement with Roosevelt, see Moley, *After Seven Years*, pp. 67–79 and 138–48.

23. Frances Fox Piven and Richard A. Cloward, *Regulating the Poor: The Functions of Public Welfare* (Tavistock Publications: London, 1972). Compare this with McElvaine, *Great Depression*.

24. Rosenman, *Roosevelt Papers*, I, pp. 639–46.

CHAPTER 3

The Early New Deal, Relief and the Pursuit of Recovery

If no clear New Deal programme had emerged during the presidential campaign, neither did a completed set of proposals emerge from the four-month interregnum. The Brain Trust ceased to meet as a group after November 1932 but individual members continued their work of preparing proposals for the President, and some cabinet appointees were already working on their own particular areas of responsibility. Since the President-elect neither said much to indicate the likely shape of his policy, nor responded to President Hoover's attempts to draw him into joint action, the sense of uncertainty within the country increased. Roosevelt did announce the names of his cabinet by stages but his choice of cabinet members did not reflect a coherent political and economic philosophy. Among the figures who played a major part in the New Deal were the Secretary of Agriculture, Henry Wallace, a man of immense experience in the farming world; Harold Ickes, the Secretary of the Interior, who brought to his administration both political influence (as an independent Republican who had supported FDR in 1932) and also a reputation for liberalism, honesty and integrity; and, one of Roosevelt's most innovative appointments, as Secretary of Labor, the first woman cabinet member in American history, Frances Perkins. Perkins had worked with Roosevelt in New York, as had Harry Hopkins, who was later appointed as head of the Federal Emergency Relief Administration (FERA). All of these figures, who between them controlled the main spending departments, were on the liberal wing of American politics. Conversely, however, the Treasury was under the control of first William Woodin, and later Henry Morgenthau Jr; both men, like the Director of the Budget, Lewis Douglas, were fiscal conservatives. Roosevelt also retained as advisers several of his Brain Trust, notably Moley and Tugwell, who were employed at Assistant Secretary rank. Although they were advocates of government-business planning of the economy, their detailed views were very different, again making it difficult to predict with any certainty the future shape of the New Deal.

None the less, discussions were taking place on policy. The programme closest to fruition by March 1933 was in agriculture, important because of the base of Roosevelt's support, but also seen as crucial to overall recovery. The two people most responsible for agricultural policy, Secretary of Agriculture Henry Wallace and Rexford Tugwell, had a lot of experience on agricultural matters, close links with academic agricultural experts, and a very competent team of economists in the Department of Agriculture ready to give assistance. The new Secretary of Labor, Frances Perkins, had a reform agenda already in mind. Her interests lay in the field of social policy and welfare, and according to her memoirs, she made plain to Roosevelt that she had a 'wish list' of social reform measures.[1] Notable by its absence, however, was any consensus on how to tackle the question of economic recovery. According to Moley, while some ideas were clearly in circulation, not only within the Brain Trust but also in other groups such as enlightened businessmen, these had not yet gathered sufficient coherence or support to justify any legislative planning.[2] It should be stressed that the President did not expect to hold a full Congressional session, and therefore there was time in hand to consolidate his recovery plans. However, one important aspect of the New Deal was already apparent – the limited overview of the economy as a whole. Individuals, both in and outside the incoming administration, were certainly active and formulating ideas, but there was no overall strategy or structure for strategic planning, other than that provided by the President. As Roosevelt took the oath of office in March 1933, there still existed no structured New Deal programme for presentation to Congress.

The new President soon ended the mood of uncertainty and inaction, however. His Administration faced a demoralized nation as well as an impoverished one. To this problem it brought the novelty and excitement of change; a variety of schemes and theories for recovery, albeit sometimes contradictory; a group of talented administrators, many of whom had pronounced humanitarian leanings; a Congress that was controlled by the same party as the Administration; and a President whose many gifts included the capacity to speak to, and captivate, ordinary Americans, despite his own privileged background. It was this last advantage that was to be utilized first, when Roosevelt addressed the nation at his inauguration. Not only was his firm and determined tone a much needed tonic, he also made plain that he intended to take decisive emergency action to address the economic crisis. This he did, the following day, when, using powers granted in the 1917 Trading with the Enemy Act, he declared a four-day national bank holiday and called Congress into immediate emergency session, to begin on 9 March.

This special session was originally designed to tackle only the bank crises which posed an immediate threat not only to the economic activity but also the social fabric of the United States. However, it became apparent within a matter of days that the scale of pressing problems outside finance also demanded a rapid response. After nearly four years of Depression, many individual Americans were literally desperate, yet access to even the most parsimonious relief was limited. Moreover, many businessmen were also in dire straits. Within days of taking office, the Administration was implored by representatives of both the coal and oil industries to take drastic action to save their industries, by a policy of nationalization if necessary.[3] Agricultural problems also demanded a rapid response. The spring and summer planting season was rapidly approaching, and there were indications of growing farmer militancy, particularly in the Farm Holiday Association, a militant group willing to take direct action to withhold agricultural produce from the markets in an attempt to stimulate action.[4] In an emergency atmosphere akin to wartime, in which all sectors of the American public appeared willing to co-operate with the new Administration, Roosevelt rapidly decided to capitalize upon the support and enthusiasm of the new Congress and extend the special session to address some of the many other pressing problems facing the nation.

The net result of this special session, which, because of its duration, is usually referred to as the Hundred Days, was a torrent of legislation; some fifteen major measures, which sought not only to stimulate recovery and tackle the financial crisis, but also to address one of the most serious problems of all – public confidence and need. Long-term reform, although of less immediate importance, also had a place in the programme. The main acts, and the dates of their passing, are set out in the Chronology. Despite the speed of their presentation to Congress (many of the bills were administration drafts, rather than originating within Congress itself), few of the measures had been drafted prior to the commencement of the special session. Initially, the main priority was to restore the nation's banking system, and the other two measures first presented to Congress consisted of an Economy Bill cutting government spending and a bill repealing prohibition – hardly indicative of a well-structured radical reform package. The remaining bills were rapidly prepared to capitalize upon a co-operative Congress, and, as a result, were often hastily, even sloppily, drafted, a problem that was ultimately to have negative repercussions for the New Deal. In addition, several of the bills were omnibus measures, incorporating a number of different policies (for example, the Agricultural Adjustment Act), or representing a compromise between several different proposals. This was notably so in the case of the National Industrial Recovery Act (NIRA), which was hastily put together in order to divert Congress from passing its own measure, which would impose a compulsory maximum 30-hour week.

In the crisis conditions prevailing as the new Congress assembled, the first priority was necessarily the banking system of the country, which was in virtual collapse. A short bank holiday might halt the immediate crisis, but this could last no more than a few days. When the banks reopened, there had to be a restoration of public confidence in their operation. An Emergency Banking Act was prepared with the close co-operation of the outgoing Treasury team, and passed, sight unseen, in a record one day. Ironically, this Act employed a legacy of the Hoover Administration, the Reconstruction Finance Corporation, which was to play a major role in the New Deal, becoming in effect the largest bank in the country. The RFC was authorized to buy bank stock and, if necessary, to assume bank debts in order to ensure their soundness. The Act also temporarily forbade the hoarding and export of gold, and suspended dollar convertibility to gold. Once the Act had been passed, the Administration worked frantically to ensure that nearly 70 per cent of the banks functioning in early March were ready to reopen once the bank holiday ended.[5] However, the question still remained as to whether the country would accept that the newly reorganized banking system was trustworthy. This was, in many ways, a particularly critical point in the fortunes of the New Deal. Had public confidence in the restructured banking system faltered, then the result would have been a financial crisis even more profound than that facing the Administration on 4 March; moreover, the authority of the new Administration would have been seriously dented. Yet again, the President's ability to capture and influence the public mood came to the fore. On 12 March, the evening before the banks reopened, in the first of his famous 'fireside chats', he spoke in straightforward language, explaining the reasons for the banking crisis in non-technical terms, and assuring the American people that any banks which reopened would be secure. It ended with the words 'Together we cannot fail'.[8] When deposits exceeded withdrawals on the next day, the success of the measure, and even more importantly, the standing and authority of the President, was demonstrated beyond doubt. In the optimistic and positive atmosphere this engendered, it is not surprising that Franklin Roosevelt decided to capitalize upon the momentum that he had created and keep the special Congress in session for longer than originally intended.

While the first banking measure enabled some reorganization, and the reopening of 'sound' banks, there was a need for further banking reform. So, also within the Hundred Days, another banking act was passed which imposed additional controls on bank officials, provided for the complete separation of commercial and investment banking, and also set up a system of federal guarantees of small bank deposits up to a maximum of $2,500. While some of the problems of the banking sector remained, notably the division between nationally and state organized institutions, these measures dramatically reduced bank failures and the loss of deposits. The other major financial institution, the Stock Exchange, was also subjected to considerable regulation, in the form of the Federal Securities Act, which required the disclosure of certain types of information to investors. A year later, in June 1934, the regulation of the Stock Exchange was further extended by the creation of the Securities and Exchange Commission, which took an active role under the 'poacher turned gamekeeper', Joseph Kennedy – one of a small band of New Deal businessmen. In regulating these financial institutions, the New Dealers had no need to fear popular opposition, as the standing of bankers and financiers was extremely low.

The main focus of the extended special session was clearly the proposals aimed at economic recovery. Two main measures were included, the National Industrial Recovery Act (NIRA) and the Agricultural Adjustment Act (AAA). The latter was accorded considerable significance since so much of the economic activity of the country was based upon farms and agribusiness, and farmers had faced depression throughout the 1920s. Many New Dealers, including Roosevelt himself, believed that the restoration of rural purchasing power held the key to industrial recovery. Both acts were prepared by a number of individuals, not necessarily working in concert; as a consequence, they tended to be an amalgam of measures, including the acceptance, in the case of the AAA, of the Thomas Amendment permitting the President to engage in various inflationary measures. A wide variety of groups and individuals were involved in the formulation of the NIRA. Accounts given by the participants vary in emphasis and even in the personnel mentioned, but it seems clear that Roosevelt had authorized a number of groups and individuals to propose industrial recovery measures. That suggested by Secretary of Labor Perkins, which essentially relied upon a programme of maximum hours and minimum wages monitored and policed by the Secretary of Labor, gained very little support, but a number of other ideas were considered by, amongst others, Rexford Tugwell, Hugh Johnson, Raymond Moley and Senator Wagner. In what was to become a characteristic New Deal response, Roosevelt told the various groups to lock themselves in a room and hammer out a compromise, which is what eventually happened.[7]

The resultant National Industrial Recovery Act sought to restore purchasing power and avoid excessive, cut-throat competition. Businessmen were encouraged to accept codes of practice which would impose prices, production levels and the quality of merchandise and services. In return, the businesses involved in the codes would be exempt from anti-trust legislation. The codes would have to be approved by a federal administrator, but would be voluntary. Given that such codes gave immense power to business, countervailing obligations were required, including minimum wages and maximum hours, the end to sweat shops and child labour, and the granting of certain rights of collective bargaining to the workers, in Section 7(a). This structure reflected the emphasis placed by many groups upon the planning of the American economy. It also drew heavily upon the experience during the First World War of the War Industries Board, as directed by financier Bernard Baruch. This indicated that the Roosevelt administration recognized the lesson of the First World War, 'that the federal government could mobilize the nation's resources in a planned economy'.[8] It provided a framework of order and regulation, and followed lines proposed by a number of enlightened businessmen, such as Gerald Swope of General Electric. Hugh Johnson, who was appointed as the first administrator of the National Recovery Administration (NRA), had had experience with the War Industries Board, and rapidly took up the challenge of winning business support and compliance. The NIRA also included a large appropriation for public works, intended to contribute to the economic recovery by stimulating the construction industry. However, the slow implementation of the public works programme, as a result of the remarkable caution of the administrator of the Public Works Administration, Harold Ickes, meant that it was not functional until into 1934.

In the case of agriculture, farmers were paid to take land out of production in certain key crops, the payments to be financed by a tax on food processing. Decisions as to allotments of acreage reduction between individual farms and the monitoring of compliance would be the responsibility of local committees of farmers, on the assumption that they would know local conditions. In its basic structure, this plan reflected the voluntary domestic allotment plan of M. L. Wilson, which both Wallace and Tugwell had supported for some time. Its main intention was to curb production, thus increasing prices, while also expanding farm income not only through the higher prices but also the AAA payments. However, there was scope for the Administration to pursue other agricultural policies, including the negotiation of marketing agreements. At the insistence of Congress, the Thomas Amendment was added to the bill, giving FDR the discretionary power to inflate the currency. The AAA was passed by 12 May 1933, thus averting a farmers' strike threatened for 13 May. It initially included only those commodities facing the greatest difficulties, notably cotton, corn, dairy farming, pigs, rice, tobacco and wheat, but it was extended to some other vulnerable crops over the next two years.

Neither of these measures represented an attempt at major reform, although the NIRA did address certain fundamental shortcomings in the working conditions in particular industries, and some of its supporters (notably Tugwell, who favoured national planning, as opposed to Moley whose emphasis was on business leadership) hoped to see planning and co-operation, rather than cut-throat competition, a permanent part of the American economy. The main goal was recovery, and in order to do this, self-regulation was encouraged. Years of campaigning against monopoly were disregarded, as businesses were encouraged to plan together.[9] Although the government was involved in the planning process, it was very much at a distance, establishing the ground rules but interfering little with the actual running of the scheme. At the heart of both the NRA and the AAA was the assumption that the fundamental problem faced was one of over-production. The answer to that was to cut supply, rather than directly enhance demand, although the payments to farmers and minimum wage provisions did restore some additional purchasing power.

In effect, then, both acts encouraged the bigger units in industry and agriculture to plan together in order to enforce scarcity and hence push up prices.[10] However, although both acts heralded a level of government intervention in the economy unprecedented in American history, they also had been framed in accordance with certain implicit constraints. Government involvement did not take the form of massive public ownership, nor of fully integrated economic planning. Both measures also made it virtually inevitable that the Administration would pursue a policy of economic nationalism, for operations in price fixing could only succeed if the American market was not at threat from international dumping. Thus, the overall assumption of the New Deal was that recovery had to be sought through domestic rather than international means. In a world-wide depression, where other industrial nations were also suffering from a loss of exports, and primary producers had seen a drop in income, any hope of finding a solution to the American Depression through increasing exports was purely illusory (although this hope helped prompt the recognition by the United States, for the first time, of the Soviet Union, which alone among developed nations appeared to escape the trauma of depression). Of the three main aspects of international economic policy, the Roosevelt administration saw no reason to modify the high tariff barriers, for allowing cheaper foreign goods into the American market would destroy any hope of raising prices through the control of agricultural and industrial production. The vexed issue of war debts and reparations effectively faded from prominence. That left only the question of fixed exchange rates between the countries of the world. In April 1933, the temporary provisions of the Emergency Banking Act were made permanent, effectively taking the United States off the gold standard, opening up the possibility of inflationary policies. However, this meant that the United States could not afford to co-operate with other countries in addressing the international economy. Hence, although an American delegation attended the World Economic Conference held in London during June and July 1933, the President effectively sabotaged it by making clear that he would not co-operate in any policy aimed at restoring fixed exchange rates. As this also undermined the position of Raymond Moley, the President's special envoy to the Conference, this began the process of Moley's disillusion-ment with the New Deal.[11]

The Administration also recognized the potential importance of credit within the economy, as a way of assisting both individual Americans and also the large credit institutions that had been affected by the banking crisis and the lack of capital investment. All the various farm credit agencies were consolidated into the Farm Credit Administration, which in eighteen months had refinanced more than 20 per cent of all farm mortgages. The Commodity Credit Corporation, operating under the auspices of the RFC, made loans against the security of surplus crops, thus providing an alternative source of credit. For individuals facing repossession of their homes as a result of the credit freeze and economic disaster, the Home Owners' Refinancing Act created a Home Owners' Loan Corporation within the RFC, which could refinance home mortgages.[12] Over the next eighteen months further measures relating to credit were passed, including the creation of a Federal Housing Administration in June 1934 to offer federal insurance on special mortgages (low-interest, long-term) for those buying new homes, thus assisting in the fields of credit and construction at the same time.

Of particular interest to the President was the issue of conservation. As one of the first initiatives in the provision of federal relief, the Civilian Conservation Corps (CCC) was formed at FDR's own instigation. The scheme, which provided residential camp placements for young jobless men aged 17–24, was funded entirely by the federal government and was probably the New Deal's most popular relief programme. The recruits were provided with board and lodging in camps across the United States and were expected to send the bulk of their monthly wages of $50 home to their families. Within two years, the CCC included half a million men, located in 2,500 camps. In one of the few long-term reform measures of the Hundred Days, the Tennessee Valley Authority (TVA) was created, offering a programme of massive regional planning, the generation of cheap electricity and social reform. The Tennessee River ran through seven of the poorest states in the United States, with a population of around two million. During the 1930s, the TVA embarked upon a comprehensive programme of flood control (the dams erected for the purpose were used to generate electricity), soil erosion programmes (notably reforestation), better farming methods such as contour ploughing and the use of fertiliser, and educational programmes. The generation of electricity, although presented as a secondary function of flood control, was clearly important as part of Roosevelt's long-standing commitment to set 'yardstick prices' when it came to public utilities.

For the unemployed and the destitute, the most directly relevant aspect of the Hundred Days was the provision of relief. The winter of 1932–3 had clearly demonstrated that the resources of both local government and private charities were overwhelmed. Hoover's attempt to address the problem by lending money to individual states had been totally insufficient. That something had to be done at federal level may appear obvious with hindsight, but few in the United States appreciated that national action was imperative. Roosevelt had, however, come close to such recognition during his New York days, and he brought with him to Washington two of his subordinates from that period: Frances Perkins, who, when appointed Secretary of Labor, had stressed the importance of providing a welfare safety net; and Harry Hopkins, the key figure in the state's Temporary Emergency Relief Administration, who later headed the New Deal's three main relief programmes, the Federal Emergency Relief Administration (FERA), the Civil Works Administration (CWA) and the Works Progress Administration (WPA). The task of providing relief was a massive one. The scale of need was reflected in October 1933, when the federal government conducted a nation-wide review. Despite the small upturn in the economy over the summer, nearly thirteen million Americans – some 10 per cent of the population – relied on relief from a public agency (as opposed to a private charity). This figure included over five million children under the age of sixteen. Moreover, those on relief were disproportionately concentrated in the industrial states and cities of the north-east and Midwest.[13] Even before the results of this survey were known, during the Hundred Days a number of different measures sought to address the problem of those in need.

As part of the NIRA, $3.3 billion was provided for public works, administered through the Public Works Administration (PWA). However, as its attachment to the NIRA demonstrated, this was regarded as predominantly a pump priming measure, to promote economic recovery, and did not have as its main function the rapid provision of employment for those already out of work. The first immediate response to the task of relief was the FERA, which worked upon the basis of joint federal-state enterprises, mainly administered through the states, thus, it was hoped, counteracting some of the constitutional difficulties involved in the provision of federal funding for relief. Harry Hopkins had at his initial disposal a total of $500 million (again provided through the ubiquitous RFC), $200 million of which was allocated to the states on the basis of previous relief expenditure (with the federal government donating one dollar for every three spent by the state) while the rest provided a fund at the disposal of the federal relief administrator to make discretionary grants. However, the reliance on state governments led to considerable discrepancies between regions. The extent of the operation was vast, for in 40 states the number on relief accounted for more than 10 per cent of the population. Under the auspices of FERA, every state created relief agencies (in June 1933 they had existed in only eight of the 48 states). FERA provided a wide range of support programmes, including food orders, direct relief, work relief and specially administered programmes for migrant workers and rural rehabilitation. Most significant of all, whatever the limitations within which it operated, FERA created a crucial precedent, that the federal government had a role to play within the provision of relief to the needy.[14]

If we analyze the various achievements of the Hundred Days in terms of the 'three Rs' (relief, recovery and reform), it is apparent that the first two goals predominated, as one might expect. Reform there was, certainly, in the TVA in particular, but also in some of the labour provisions of the NIRA. However, the emphasis was on immediate relief of suffering and the instigation of recovery measures. In looking back at the first three months of the New Deal, it is difficult to discern any coherent philosophy. The acts passed were an amalgam of often improvised programmes, and some of the measures, for example, the Economy Act, were in clear contradiction of others. There are, none the less, certain clear patterns: the economic rationale underlying the NIRA and the AAA was reasonably similar; banking and the stock exchange were carefully regulated; and there was a humanitarian intention to ensure that relief was given to those Americans most in need, regardless of constitutional limitations. One striking feature of many of the acts was the sweeping powers given to the President to act at his own discretion; for example, to approve codes set up under NRA. It can be argued that the attempt to address the problems of a wide number of groups, and to create countervailing balances of power, was pluralist in intent, creating a broker state, with Roosevelt as the honest broker. In many instances there was a clear resonance of the wartime years, when emergency needs had brought the American people together, prompted the service of businessmen in Washington, encouraged capital and labour to work together (albeit with guaranteed rights to labour) and emphasized the importance of the nation over sectional interests. The rhetoric of war was clearly evident within the New Deal at this time, and historian William Leuchtenburg has clearly delineated what he sees as the 'analogue of war' during its first years.[15] In addition, the sheer excitement of the Hundred Days generated a sense of optimism and change. Leuchtenburg himself, then a boy of ten, clearly recalled the excitement of the early days of the Roosevelt administration: 'I was caught up in the irresistible pace of the First Hundred Days with headlines of newly created alphabet agencies conveying the ineluctable excitement about national politics'.[16]

However, the legislation passed in Washington was only the first step. The ultimate shape of the New Deal would depend upon the thousands of administrators who put the programmes into practice, devised the individual schemes and proposed amendments and refinements to the hastily drafted legislation. This posed an immense challenge to the Administration, faced with the need to staff and implement a number of wide-ranging programmes, many of them requiring considerable bureaucratic input. To some extent this was helped by the proviso in both the NIRA and the FERA that the posts created under the measures were to be exempt from the Civil Service requirements. Even so, the mission of providing enough administrators was no light matter. To handle the vast task of local administration of schemes such as FERA, the PWA, the NRA, the AAA, etc., a number of expedients were followed. The AAA drew heavily upon the existing expertise of the Department of Agriculture Extension Service, while the FERA used local administrators already in place and also turned to the pool of talent within private charities. In the case of the NRA, the lack of government expertise encouraged the use of businessmen to manage the codes of fair competition. However, as will be discussed in a later chapter, this diversity had mixed consequences for the American people.

With regard to the main recovery measures, an Agricultural Adjustment Administration was created with George Peek as chief administrator. By the time that it was in place, however, the important spring period was past, and it was therefore necessary to take emergency measures, including the ploughing-up of ten million acres of cotton and the slaughter of six million pigs. There was a cruel irony in the destruction of food and cotton when many Americans were malnourished and in need of clothing. However, this is a clear reflection of the continued emphasis on the capitalist ethos underpinning the New Deal, with respect for market forces and property rights. In addition, the Government encouraged the negotiation of marketing agreements between growers and processors in certain industries (tobacco, for example). The main priority then was to fix quotas as rapidly as possible for the 1934 and 1935 seasons, with the goal of reducing production by 20–40 per cent; soon local committees began to operate, and individual farmers signed contracts promising to reduce their acreage. By the spring of 1934, there were over 4,000 local committees, covering more than three million farmers. This efficiency owed much to the existence, through the Department of Agriculture's Extension Service, of a ready-made nation-wide administration, and to the considerable expertise existing within the Department of Agriculture.[17] Inevitably, however, problems developed. There was an inbuilt tension between the interests of the producers, who wished for higher prices, and consumers, to whom the food processors passed on the additional tax costs. An indirect approach to production control, such as that adopted by the AAA, could be circumvented in a number of ways. Thus, for example, with the use of fertilisers, machinery and improved production techniques, a smaller amount of land could actually result in a larger total output. In other cases, such as that of cotton, there already existed in storage from previous years more than enough cotton to meet the 1933 demand. The Commodity Credit Corporation helped mitigate the impact of the massive surpluses. Indeed, for many commercial farmers the most significant measures of the New Deal were those addressing problems of credit and indebtedness.

Not all farmers were owner-occupiers, however, and the AAA did not address the needs of all tenant farmers. Monies paid for the taking of land out of production often did not reach the tenant farmers, thus increasing their financial difficulties. Moreover, in the particular circumstances of the South, difficulties soon developed over the relationship between the landowner and his tenant farmers, particularly those with the peculiarly Southern status of sharecropper.[18] Sometimes the entire landholding of an individual sharecropper was designated to lie fallow, amounting to virtual eviction. The AAA essentially strengthened the position of the large farmers and landowners at the expense of the sharecroppers. Attempts to protest against this in the South, through the creation of a bi-racial Southern Tenant Farmers' Union with the support of the Socialist Party, met with little success and much repression. The plight of share-croppers did not pass unnoticed. A number of young lawyers within the AAA's Legal Department sought to provide protection for tenant farmers, but succeeded only in bringing about their own dismissal.[19] It became clear that the AAA could not be expected to undertake reform of the worst social evils in American agriculture. In terms of recovery, however, it did have some effect; although it is difficult to separate the consequences of government policy from the impact upon production of the drought conditions which hit the 'dustbowl' of the Great Plains during 1934 and 1935.

For many New Dealers, the key to overall economic recovery lay on the farm, but it was, of course, vital to promote industrial recovery. At first sight, it appeared as though policies directed to this end would be slow off the ground. The PWA was particularly prone to delay, thanks to Ickes's determination to ensure personally that the highest standards of probity prevailed. Moreover, large public works programmes required a long lead-in time. In the first six months, only $110 million of the $3.3 billion appropriation was spent, and by then the forthcoming winter meant that few new projects would be introduced until the following spring. The NRA, which administered the industry codes, was under the directorship of General Hugh Johnson. For it to retain credibility, it was critical that Johnson enlist the support of at least the ten largest industries. As a man of immense enthusiasm, if at times intemperate, he threw himself into the task, but initially it appeared far from promising. Although the general plans of the NRA reflected ideas current in some business circles, there was still considerable suspicion at the idea of federal regulation, and also concern at the imposition of particular working practices and collective bargaining. Initially the NRA had to resort to the President's Re-employment Agreement by which individual companies agreed to retain their labour force while maintaining wages and keeping prices stable. By dint of an evangelical-style publicity campaign, centred around the symbol of the NRA (a Blue Eagle), Johnson secured over two million agreements, covering over sixteen million employees. The pervasiveness of the symbol of the Blue Eagle was considerable. In a film issued in 1933, *Footlight Parade,* the two stars, James Cagney and Ruby Keeler, appeared in the finale holding aloft placards depicting the Blue Eagle and also the image of FDR.[20] After the initial reluctance, Johnson was later able to secure the support of many major industries, assisted by the dawning recognition that the powers given to business were quite considerable. Indeed, he succeeded almost too well. In all, 557 codes were eventually adopted, covering 90 per cent of the nation's industrial capacity. The task of administering and monitoring so many codes pushed the NRA to the limit, and allowed scope for corruption, collusion and cartelization. This was later to have serious consequences. Business also proved adept at circumventing the provisions relating to labour, particularly collective bargaining. While organized labour had hailed Section 7(a) as a Magna Carta and had seized the opportunity to launch a recruiting drive, many firms were quick to organize company unions, denying the spirit if not the letter of the legislation. Attempts by the

Administration to counter this, through the setting up of a National
Labor Board and later, in the summer of 1934, a National Labor Relations
Board to control unfair labour practices, failed due to the vague nature of
the original legislation. Conversely, however, conditions undoubtedly
improved for many workers, who saw hours cut and wages increased,
and child labour was largely eradicated, at least in the industrial sector. It
has been estimated that the NRA was responsible for as much as a 26 per
cent annual increase in wages during its short tenure. The testimony of
individual Americans emphasizes how considerable the impact of the
NRA had been. 'Before NRA I worked 7 a.m. to 10 or 11 p.m. Now two of
us work 8 hours a day each.' 'Without NRA the undersigned [over 100
workers] would be out of jobs and our children back in the mill.'[21]

By the autumn of 1933, therefore, most of the main programmes were
up and running. However, whereas after June 1933 the main legislative
impulse slowed somewhat, it was clearly insufficient for the New Dealers
to remain content with the framework created during the Hundred Days.
Although some time had to be allowed for the initial torrent of legislation
to be absorbed and put into practice, inevitably omissions and flaws in the
original acts required action, while unfolding events required continuous
responses. So, although the next major instalment of legislation did not
come until 1935, before that a number of new bills and measures were
introduced. The most significant in the field of relief was the formation of
the Civil Works Administration (CWA) to supplement, and in many
cases replace, the work of FERA. By the autumn it was clear that FERA
alone would be insufficient to tide the country over the approaching
winter, given the lack of any substantial economic upturn. From
November 1933 to March 1934, therefore, Hopkins was responsible for
the CWA, a purely federal programme, which had at its disposal $400
million from the slow-moving PWA. This was a marked departure from
all precedents in work relief, and indeed was unique within the New
Deal. CWA workers were simply that – employees of the federal
government – and the psychological, as well as the financial, benefits
were immense. The agency transferred two million 'work reliefers' from
FERA. The other two million were recruited by the new United States
Employment Service, also created during the Hundred Days, on the basis
of skill and experience, not need. There was no means test, several
members of one family could be employed at the same time, the wage
rates paid were at the hourly rate prevailing in PWA schemes (even if the
number of hours was curtailed), employees were covered by workmen's

compensation legislation and above all they were paid in cash. Moreover, it was a federally funded and directed scheme although it still had to work through state relief boards and existing local expertise to a large extent. Although the programme undoubtedly had its fair share of 'made work' it also achieved much in its brief existence, building or improving 500,000 miles of roads, 40,000 schools, over 3,500 parks and playgrounds, and 1,000 airports. Moreover, in a foretaste of the imaginative provision of white-collar work relief under the WPA it also hired teachers, nurses, artists, architects and actors.[22] However, it proved too expensive and generated fears that public relief might prove too great a threat to private wage levels, so after the worst of the winter was over, it was steadily phased out during the spring of 1934. Not only did criticism of CWA abound, including accusations that the 'work' relief was manufactured, unnecessary and scrimped, but FDR was also unwilling to travel too far down the path of massive, deficit-financed expenditures.

Much of the remaining legislation during 1934 related to the economy. The economic nationalism of the Hundred Days was undermined slightly by the Reciprocal Trade Agreements Act of 12 June 1934. This Act authorized the President to negotiate agreements with other nations for the reciprocal raising or lowering of tariffs by up to 50 per cent. The Secretary of State, Cordell Hull, was known to advocate such a policy, but its effects were comparatively limited, being confined mainly to Latin America, and it is likely that the main effect of the various agreements reached was political rather than economic. The other two critical areas were agriculture and finance. As can be seen from the Chronology, in agriculture, there were further measures to improve the provision of credit to farmers and assist creditors in rural communities. The provisions of the AAA were extended to additional commodities. In terms of currency and finance, FDR turned to the panacea of inflation, a popular remedy for economic depression throughout American history. The farmers of the South and West, so important in Roosevelt's election, were particularly strong advocates of such a measure. During the Hundred Days, FDR had resisted attempts to force his hand on inflation but he had refused to rule it out altogether. However, in the face of growing agrarian and labour discontent, the calls for inflationary measures grew ever stronger, and therefore he embarked on a number of schemes, made possible by the departure of the American dollar from the gold standard in April 1933. A number of measures were adopted. In October 1933 the RFC was authorized to buy gold at a price which was changed from day to day in order to deter speculators. The Silver Purchase Act placated those calling for the remonetization of silver (although this never occurred) as well as winning the support of the politically important far western silver producing states. In January 1934 the Gold Reserve Act pegged the price of gold at $35 an ounce, whereas at the beginning of the New Deal in March 1933 it had stood at $20.67. In effect, then, the dollar had been devalued by nearly 60 per cent. The gold buying schemes, the Silver Purchase Act and the devaluation of the dollar and daily setting of a new gold price all basically incorporated a policy of inflation, albeit with little impact on overall economic performance. Even if economically unsuccessful, however, they served to divert potentially strong areas of political opposition, such as the silver producing states of the far west, as well as popular discontent.

This may be an appropriate point at which to study the consequences of some of the early New Deal measures. The most disappointing failure, not least because in many ways it was the area most crucial to the recovery from the Depression, was the NRA itself. In this, as with the task of overall economic recovery, the New Deal ultimately failed. Despite the immense amount of effort put into the organization and structure of the NRA codes and publicity drives, it proved unpopular with both the general public and the businesses it sought to help, even though many of its individual measures, particularly in terms of labour protection, proved very popular with workers. Indeed, at a later stage in the New Deal, those labour provisions were incorporated into permanent law, through the Wagner Act and the Fair Labor Standards Act. However, the increased prices which resulted were more the product of price fixing than the alignment of supply and demand; farmers found their gains in prices for agricultural commodities undermined by increased industrial prices; and workers were disillusioned by the ease with which many employers circumvented the collective bargaining provisions of Section 7(a). Workers were represented in only 37 of the 450 code authorities approved in the first year of the NRA's activities, and small businesses were underrepresented. Consumers were also concerned at rising prices and suspicions grew that businesses were using the scheme to their own advantage. This conclusion was reinforced by the National Recovery Review Board set up by Congress in March 1934, otherwise known as the Darrow Commission of Enquiry and highly critical of the NRA. Even business, which in so many ways benefited from the stability, price increases and planning potential of the NRA, expressed concerns through such organizations as the National Association of Manufacturers and the Chamber of Commerce. For many, the costs in terms of government intervention, and in particular labour concessions, were too high. This was a not uncommon trend. In looking at the coal industry, Frances Perkins commented that the very mine owners who had begged the federal government to nationalize their mines in the spring of 1933, began to resent the regulation implicit in the NRA once prices and demand began to improve.[23] Although there was a slight upturn in the economy in the summer of 1933, and it is calculated that in the period between June and October 1933 around two million of the unemployed found jobs, thereafter the pace of recovery slowed.

Similarly, in agriculture, the effects of the AAA were not as great as had been hoped, although the administration of the agricultural programme proved more effective than the industrial equivalent. Prices did increase, but the attempt to curb production by restricting land use was flawed, and as a consequence a number of other expedients had had to be adopted, such as the extension of loans on crops. Moreover, while urban dwellers resented the increase in prices which resulted from the improved crop prices and the tax on the food processing industry, farmers in turn found that the prices which they had to pay for the goods which they bought offset some of the gains from the AAA. Both the AAA and the NRA relied upon individual co-operation in voluntary schemes which, in effect, had to deliver clear advantages in order to retain that co-operation. While the farmers showed no sign of withdrawing their co-operation, as many businessmen had done, neither were they prepared to abide by the spirit of the AAA by genuinely restricting production. Moreover, the AAA did nothing to ease the plight of the many rural poor. This was, of course, because few of those involved in the administration of agricultural policy regarded the issue of social reform as significant. This merely strengthened the impression that in both the main recovery programmes, working as they did within the capitalist system, the federal government could only rely upon a limited pattern of co-operation.

In the immediate aftermath of the Hundred Days, signs of economic improvement and the introduction of the relief programmes were sufficient to create a positive upsurge in popular morale. However, by the autumn of 1933, the signs of economic upturn had stopped while unemployment remained at over ten million (as it was to do so throughout 1934 and 1935). As matters continued to be difficult over the next winter, with no obvious signs of improvement on the way, opposition grew. As is often the case, limited improvement brought more protest than no improvement at all. The growing discontent was expressed in street, labour and agrarian form. The commercial farmers were expressing discontent, while there was growing militancy among the Southern Tenant Farmers' Union. Continued organization among the unemployed and those on relief alarmed some, particularly since Communists were prominent within the leadership. Moreover, 1934 saw a number of outbreaks of labour militancy. The San Francisco long-shoremen's strike, the Minnesota general strike and numerous other strikes seeking recognition for unions from hitherto intransigent employers, many accompanied by widespread popular support, were all indicative of growing rank-and-file protest. Nearly 1.5 million workers participated in strikes in 1934. There was a growing assertion of a sense of values which rejected untrammelled market forces, and asserted that the skewed distribution of wealth was unfair and should be redressed. At its most basic level, this was manifested through spontaneous action to nullify the effects of forced foreclosure sales of farms, and also complaints and protests at the termination of the CWA.[24] Complaints against the NRA also increased. Essentially, the NRA had lost – if it had ever enjoyed – the social consensus that its original framers had hoped would underpin a voluntary system. This meant, however, that there was no industrial programme in operation that enlisted the support of the American people. While radicalism increased, and complaints about New Deal programmes grew, even those on relief apparently lost their initial gratitude at receiving any assistance; there were growing reports of reliefers becoming more aggressive and truculent, more ready to complain at perceived (or real) injustices and inequities. This was recognized by FDR in a fireside chat of 28 June 1934, in which he attempted both to point out improvements through his central theme – 'Are you better off than you were last year?' – and also to imply that those criticizing progress were seeking special political or financial privilege.[25] The very nature of this speech suggested that Roosevelt was being forced on to the political defensive.

Thus, after an initial flush of enthusiasm and apparent recovery, the New Deal appeared to be losing its way, at least at the federal level. We should beware of overemphasizing this; after all, the Democrats had won an increased majority in the Congressional elections of 1934, and FDR personally enjoyed immense popularity and prestige. Many in the Administration were working steadily on major measures that were coming close to fruition, such as proposals for social security and further regulation of the financial sector. But, as the planning approach so strongly advocated by many in the early days of the New Deal appeared discredited, as opposition to aspects of the New Deal grew among the American people, and as economic performance continued to be poor, a politician as shrewd as FDR had reason to be concerned. Economically, the New Deal was not particularly successful and appeared to be losing its central thrust; politically, as we shall see in the next chapter, it was under threat from a number of directions and there was a real danger that the President would lose ground to other, more dynamic, figures. Little could be done about the economy, it would appear, within the limits set by the Administration itself, but the political dimension was another proposition. By early 1935 the emphasis on relief and recovery within the New Deal was increasingly accompanied by reform initiatives.

Notes

1. Frances Perkins, *The Roosevelt I Knew* (Viking Press: New York, 1946), pp. 151–2.
2. Moley, *After Seven Years*, pp. 184–5.
3. Perkins, *The Roosevelt I Knew*, pp. 227–31; and Harold L. Ickes, *The Secret Diary of Harold L. Ickes* (3 vols, Simon and Schuster: New York, 1953–54), I, pp. 9–12.
4. The best study of this is J. L. Shover, *Cornbelt Rebellion: The Farmers' Holiday Association* (University of Illinois Press: Urbana, 1965).
5. For an account by a participant, emphasizing the conservative nature of the legislation, see Moley, *After Seven Years*, pp. 146–56. For banking reform more generally, see Helen M. Burns, *The American Banking Community and New Deal Banking Reforms, 1933–1935* (Greenwood Press: Westport, Connecticut, 1974).
6. Fireside Chat, 12 March 1933, Rosenman, *Roosevelt Papers*, 2, pp. 61–5.
7. Accounts by participants may be found in Moley, *After Seven Years*, pp. 184–91; Rexford Tugwell, *The Democratic Roosevelt* (Doubleday: Garden City, New York, 1957), pp. 280–6; and Perkins, *The Roosevelt I Knew*, pp. 197–212. A useful account of the origins of the NIRA may be found in Donald R. Brand, *Corporatism and the Rule of Law: A Study of the National Recovery Administration* (Cornell University Press: Ithaca, 1988), pp. 99–104.
8. William E. Leuchtenburg, *The FDR Years: On Roosevelt and his Legacy* (Columbia University Press: New York, 1995), p. 40.
9. Many historians portray the NRA as corporatist, including Colin Gordon in his book *New Deals: Business, Labor, and Politics in America, 1920–1935* (Cambridge University Press: New York, 1994). However, Brand, *Corporatism and the Rule of Law*, questions this interpretation.
10. For a discussion of the general economic policy of the Hundred Days, see William J. Barber, *Designs within Disorder: Franklin D. Roosevelt, the Economists, and the Shaping of American Economic Policy, 1933–1945* (Cambridge University Press: Cambridge, 1996), pp. 23–35.

11. Moley resigned from office on 7 September 1933, although he continued to act as an informal speechwriter and adviser for a further two years.
12. This had some similarities with Hoover's policies, except that it had $2 billion available, instead of $125 million, and was permitted to lend a higher percentage of the valuation.
13. Bonnie Fox Schwartz, *The Civil Works Administration, 1933–34: The Business of Emergency Employment in the New Deal* (Princeton University Press: Princeton, 1984), p. 3.
14. The fullest study of FERA is William R. Brock, *Welfare, Democracy, and the New Deal* (Cambridge University Press: Cambridge, 1988).
15. William E. Leuchtenburg, 'The New Deal and the Analogue of War', in *The FDR Years*, pp. 35–75.
16. Leuchtenburg, *The FDR Years.*, p. xvi.
17. The significance of this existing expertise, when compared with the NRA's reliance upon businessmen, is discussed in Kenneth Finegold and Theda Skocpol, *State and Party in America's New Deal* (University of Wisconsin Press: Madison, Wisconsin, 1995).
18. Sharecroppers were tenants who paid rent in kind (a proprortion of the crop) rather than in cash. As a consequence, they were compelled to grow commercial crops rather than following subsistence farming.
19. See Donald H. Grubbs, *Cry from the Cotton: The Southern Tenant Farmers' Union and the New Deal* (University of North Carolina Press: Chapel Hill, 1971).
20. McElvaine, *The Great Depression*, p. 214. McElvaine uses film to great effect in his book.
21. M. D. Vincent and Beulah Amidon, 'N.R.A.: A Trial Balance', *Survey Graphic* (July 1935), pp. 333–7 and 363–4, reprinted in Frank B. Freidel (ed.), *The New Deal and the American People* (Prentice-Hall: Englewood Cliffs, New Jersey, 1964), pp. 43–6.
22. A full acount of the CWA may be found in Schwartz, *The Civil Works Administration*.
23. Perkins, *The Roosevelt I Knew*, pp. 231–2.
24. Schwartz, *The Civil Works Administration*, pp. 196–212 and McElvaine, *The Great Depression*, pp. 196–249.
25. Fireside Chat, 28 June 1934; Rosenman, *Roosevelt Papers*, 3, pp. 312–18.

CHAPTER 4

The Later New Deal and Reform

By late 1934, two different factors were influencing the evolution of the New Deal. After the initial period, primarily dedicated to recovery and relief, it was possible for members of the Administration to take stock, and consider proposals for more permanent reform. The task of drafting a social security measure that would meet constitutional requirements had proved a difficult one, but by late 1934 the work of the President's Cabinet Committee on Economic Security (created in June 1934) was nearing completion. In the Department of Agriculture, there was a strong lobby, led by Rexford Tugwell, which recognized the need for more reform to be addressed not to commercial agriculture but to the appalling living conditions of sharecroppers and poorer tenant farmers. On financial issues, many advocated greater regulation of the stock exchange, while the work of reforming the banking laws was also not yet completed. Others advocated action against the monopolistic power of the largest holding companies, particularly in the power industry. The taxation system continued to rest principally on sales taxes and other indirect taxes, while the wealthiest men and companies in the country proved adept at escaping their liabilities. These last matters particularly exercised a group of advisers within the New Deal, grouped around Justice Louis Brandeis and Felix Frankfurter, who wished to restore more competition into the American economy. The best-known advocates of these views in the Administration were Benjamin Cohen and Thomas Corcoran, whose reputation as superb draftsmen of technical bills dated back to the Security Act of 1933, but whose standing was undoubtedly growing throughout 1934 and particularly 1935. Within Congress, Senator Wagner was eager to see the permanent consolidation of the gains made by organized labour under Section 7(a). All of these approaches built upon initiatives which had been put in place long since, but which had not seemed appropriate, or were not politically feasible, at an earlier point in the New Deal.

Meanwhile, from a political point of view, it was also imperative that Roosevelt and his administration should seize the initiative. Not only were there manifestations of popular discontent, as was demonstrated in Chapter 3, but support was growing for more radical politicians. At state level, a number of governors and mayors, such as Floyd Olsen, the La Follettes and Fiorello LaGuardia, threatened to surpass the Washington administration in their radicalism. Although not a major force at federal level, in 1934 the Progressive Party succeeded in winning a seat in both the Senate and the House of Representatives, while the Farmer-Laborites had not only a Senator but also three Congressmen to uphold their viewpoint. In California, novelist Upton Sinclair had won the Democratic primary election for governor with his EPIC (End Poverty in California) programme. At national level, the support generated by the three main demagogues, Father Charles Coughlin, Huey Long and Dr Francis Townsend, suggested that there might well be mass support for the introduction of some sort of welfare system at national level. Moreover, the new Congress elected in 1934 was to the left of the earlier one; not only did the Democrats make net gains, almost unheard of in a mid-term election for the governing party, but many of the new Senators and Congressmen were more radical than the Administration. If the Depression had demonstrated the failures in social provision within the United States, in marked contrast to other industrial states, the first half of 1935 suggested that there was an opportunity to incorporate safeguards against the vicissitudes of everyday life into the role of the federal government, despite traditional assumptions that such provision should rather be made at local or state level.

The growing influence of, and support for, the demagogues reflected both tendencies, for if their various programmes suggested that many Americans were willing to countenance provision of welfare and redistribution of wealth at a federal level, their mounting support increased pressure upon the Roosevelt administration to recapture the political initiative. The demagogues advocated a number of panaceas which offered dramatic, simple and supposedly fast-acting responses to economic difficulty. There is no doubt that their plans were economically unworkable, but at the time the American public greeted with enthusiasm such ideas as Townsend's Revolving Pension Scheme and Huey Long's Share Our Wealth. The first Townsend clubs, Huey Long's Share Our Wealth movement and Reverend Charles Coughlin's National Union for Social Justice were all formed in 1934. Dr Francis Townsend's proposal for economic recovery was based upon the payment of a $200 monthly pension to all those over 60, provided that the whole sum was spent within the month. The required funds would be raised by a 2 per cent sales tax. The enthusiasm which he engendered swept the elderly population of the United States, and Congress was inundated by petitions demanding the payment of pensions.

The other two demagogues appealed to a broader constituency. Huey Long, the charismatic Senator from Louisiana (commonly known as the Kingfish), similarly proposed a scheme which was shaky on economic grounds but which gathered widespread support, particularly among the impoverished farmers of the South. He proposed to redistribute the wealth of the richest in American society by imposing a strict limit on capital ownership. With the funds thus liberated, he would ensure a basic minimum income. Every family would have a capital sum of $5,000 and a guaranteed minimum income of $2,500, while the wealthy would be restricted to a capital of no more than five million dollars, and annual earnings would be capped at $5,000. The Reverend Charles Coughlin, on the other hand, had a strong following among the urban working classes of the North and Midwest. Another charismatic leader, he displayed a mastery of the radio, and soon attracted a massive audience of between 30 million and 40 million each week. Originally a supporter of Roosevelt, he advocated the nationalization of banking, credit and currency together with the remonetization of silver. Soon he turned against the Administration. By the spring of 1935, a time when the New Deal appeared to be in the doldrums, and economic recovery was proving extremely elusive, all three movements were beginning to gather pace and were demonstrating their power to mobilize public opinion, in the form of mailing campaigns to Congress, for example. All three implied that money was in too short supply and called for a redistributive programme and/or federal government control over economic forces. Long and Coughlin both focused an attack on the very wealthy bankers and financiers. All three movements appealed primarily to groups largely untouched by the New Deal – the old, fundamentalists, and lower-class Southern whites.[1]

The demagogues were taken seriously by the Roosevelt administration for a number of reasons. First, they represented the desire of Americans to find a quick, simple and politically appealing solution to the Depression, but one that was solidly rooted within the American system. They suggested that the inflationary sentiment within the United States was still strong; and indicated the level of popular hostility to the very

wealthy groups in society, the ones whom Roosevelt was later to casti-
gate as economic royalists. There was also a political threat posed by the
demagogues. The programmes offered by the three men, although
widely different in emphasis, had enough in common to make it feasible
that the three groups might align for electoral purposes (as their
organizations indeed did in 1936). Moreover, their potential appeal was
complementary. Thus, Coughlin had a lot of support from Catholics in
the industrial heartlands of the North East, whereas Long was strong in
the South and rural Midwest. Long was an effective public speaker, at a
populist level; Coughlin made superb use of the radio, a medium as yet
mastered by few politicians (with the notable exception of Franklin
Roosevelt). Huey Long represented a particularly strong threat, one
which both Roosevelt and his political manager, Jim Farley, took extremely seriously. Should Long decide to run as a third party candidate in
1936, Farley estimated that he might win sufficient votes to threaten
FDR's re-election.[2] The depth of the Administration's concern at Long's
political ambitions was clearly demonstrated, not only by their desire to
'steal Huey's thunder', but also by clear attempts to undermine him
politically and reveal his corruption and tight control over Louisiana.
Thus, the Administration withheld federal patronage from Long,
launched investigations into his tax affairs and suspended PWA projects
in Louisiana. However, it is difficult to say how far Long would have
been prepared to go in his ruthless drive for political success as he was
assassinated in September 1935.

Faced with political opposition, economic stalemate and popular discontent, at the very beginning of 1935, Roosevelt and the New Dealers
moved more positively towards reform, not only in the field of welfare
provision, as urged by Secretary Perkins, but across a wider remit. In his
State of the Union address, in January 1935, FDR called for social reform,
with the emphasis on social security and employment. He argued that 'we
have not weeded out the overprivileged and we have not effectively lifted
up the underprivileged.'[3] His administration secured a massive emergency relief appropriation of $4.8 billion in April, the formation of the
WPA in the same month, and also the creation of two agencies intended
to promote long-term rural reform, the Resettlement Administration
(RA) and the Rural Electrification Administration (REA) (1 and 11 May
respectively). The WPA provided work relief for some of the unemployed on the relief rolls, while the Social Security bill, presented to
Congress in January 1935, was intended to provide assistance for the

'unemployables' currently drawing relief (that is, the old, the disabled and families with dependent children). The Resettlement Administration, under the leadership of Rexford Tugwell, deliberately sought to address the needs of groups of the rural population largely neglected by the AAA. Thus, by the spring of 1935, there were clear indications of a new reform agenda emerging within the administration.

However, Congress thereafter began to drag its feet. Little major legislation was forthcoming in what promised to be a particularly abortive session and the President himself appeared to be losing any sense of direction, much to the dismay of the reformers within the administration. It was at this point, on 27 May 1935, that the Supreme Court delivered a major blow to the New Deal, by ruling in the Schechter decision that the NIRA was unconstitutional.[4] The demise of the NRA was not necessarily disastrous. It had lost much of its credibility, was unpopular with large groups of Americans and had little to contribute to economic recovery. However, it was a psychological blow to the prestige of the Administration. It also raised severe doubts about the likely Court response to other New Deal legislation since, in a sweeping unanimous vote, it had criticized both the definition of interstate commerce upon which the NRA had been based and the unacceptable delegation of power from the legislature to the executive. This meant that other acts dating back to the hurried Hundred Days might well suffer the same fate (as indeed did happen, in January 1936, to the Agricultural Adjustment Act), and even cast doubt upon the more carefully crafted bills now before Congress. Above all, however, if FDR was to regain the political initiative, he had to act swiftly.

It was Congress which bore the immediate brunt of the Supreme Court's action. Demanding that both Houses remain in session through the steamy Washington summer, the President made plain that they must pass certain key bills before he would accept an adjournment. His first list of 'must' bills included the administration-sponsored Social Security, Banking and Holding Company bills; but to these he added Senator Wagner's National Labor Relations bill, in which the Administration had hitherto shown little interest. A few days later, he added a fifth measure to the list; a 'soak the rich' tax scheme. In a short but intense period of activity, usually referred to as the Second Hundred Days, Congress passed all measures, albeit with amendments to the Revenue or Wealth Tax Act. It also implemented the Guffey–Snyder Act, designed to provide a replacement for the NRA code within the coal industry, and the Connally

Hot Oil Act to assist the oil industry. Both measures could be justified on the grounds of conservation of important natural resources (although the former was declared unconstitutional in May 1936 on the grounds that coal-mining was not interstate commerce). There was not, however, and never was to be, a comprehensive replacement for the NIRA, which had largely outlived its usefulness. Not only had it failed to deliver any substantial economic recovery, but its pro-business emphasis was ill at ease with the Roosevelt administration's growing disillusionment and poor relations with business. Instead of emphasizing a restriction of production to meet a restricted demand, the Roosevelt administration thereafter sought to increase consumption through the provision of relief payments, the welfare spending net and policies intended to maintain wage levels.

The measures implemented in the Second Hundred Days were largely designed to have a permanent effect upon the socio-economic system prevailing in the United States, therefore justifying a detailed survey. A major plank in the Administration's programme, and one which even relatively conservative advisers such as Moley accepted should be passed, was a social security act. However, this was complicated by the constitutional constraints imposed upon the federal government. It had been generally assumed that social concerns lay within the domain of the states, rather than Washington. It was for this reason that the Attorney General, Homer Cummings, was included within the Cabinet Committee on Economic Security, and his office's advice was sought on this difficult point. In addition, Frances Perkins consulted the aged, if liberal, Supreme Court Justice, Louis Brandeis. Nevertheless, the New Deal did not permit such considerations to undermine the determination to implement some kind of social or economic security system. Hence, many advisers to the committee urged that the implementation of individual state schemes should be built into the bill. It was also felt that such a system would permit experimentation with different schemes.[5]

As against that, however, many states would have real constitutional or political difficulties in raising sufficient funds for such a scheme; moreover, coverage would be varied and patchy. By far the best method of raising funds would be to utilize the existing, and unchallenged, taxing powers of the federal government, and this was eventually done through a payroll tax. However, contributions to an approved state system of unemployment insurance could be offset against such a tax. This provided an element of distance between the federal and state aspects of the scheme, ensuring that even if the federal section were found unconstitutional, state schemes would remain in place. One assumption underlying this approach was that once a scheme was in operation and contributions had been made, states would be unable to terminate them, even if the federal compulsion was removed. It was for this reason that the committee finally decided upon a federal-state system for unemployment insurance, although there had been arguments that an entirely federal system would be far more efficient and a better reflection of the national nature of the labour market. Old age insurance was managed by the federal government on a contributory basis, since any individual, in the course of a career, might well work within a number of different states. However, the old age compensation scheme, which aimed at providing for the needy old, and programmes for the handicapped, used the federal-state system.

The other government-sponsored measures of the Second Hundred Days addressed finance and investment, and continued the trend towards greater regulation and disclosure reflected in earlier acts. The attempt to curb holding companies in the public utilities was a limited approach to the prevalence of large corporations, but indicated a shift in direction from planning to regulation of business. The device by which a pyramid of holding companies was erected, thus justifying a massive price differential between the costs of providing the public utility and the price for which it was ultimately sold, had long been suspect. More controversial was the so-called 'death sentence' which allowed the Government to eliminate holding companies which could not prove that their existence served the cause of economic efficiency. This clause was subsequently modified to place the burden of proof on the Government, but only after intense lobbying by the utilities. In the event, the measure did a great deal to promote efficiency and rationalization within the industry. To those contemporaries who saw in the New Deal a campaign against the wealthy, the Revenue Act further confirmed their fears. It proposed federal inheritance and gift taxes, a higher personal income tax at the highest levels, an excess profits tax and a graduated corporate income tax. This, however, was intended less as a redistributive measure but rather a means of increasing government revenue to attack the growing budget deficit. The measure was considerably watered down in Congress, with the removal of the excess profits and inheritance taxes, without much protest from the Administration. However, it did represent a clear attempt to increase the taxes on the wealthiest of individuals (those earning over $50,000 per annum) who often escaped income tax while the poorest in society were paying large indirect sales taxes. The act increased the percentage of tax paid on personal income for the top band, raised taxes on large corporations and boosted estate tax. However, while there was considerable disquiet, not to mention vociferous protest from the wealthier groups in society, in fact the act did virtually nothing to redistribute income, which remained badly skewed.[6] Meanwhile, another piece of 'must' legislation, the Banking Act, gave more power to the Federal Reserve Board, and also increased government control, over the banking sector. As a consequence the heart of banking policy moved from New York to Washington DC.

The final piece of 'must' legislation was a measure which, although not drafted by the Administration, is still seen as an important part of the New Deal's achievements. The Wagner Act incorporated into the law of the land permanent gains for organized labour, ensuring that every worker had the right to collective bargaining, providing mechanisms for discerning the work-force's chosen bargaining agent and formulating the notion of 'fair labour practices' to prevent the worst excesses of unscrupulous employers. A National Labor Relations Board, with enforcement powers, was created to monitor the act. The original assumption had been that the hand of the unions would have to be strengthened against the 'company unions' so often advocated by employers. Instead, however, the Board often found itself adjudicating the internecine feud between the American Federation of Labor (AFL) and the newly formed Committee for Industrial Organization (CIO), which for the most part included unions covering the new mass production industries. Under the auspices of the act, and, even more significantly, the rise of rank-and-file militancy aimed at securing union recognition within the main industries such as steel and automobiles, union membership in the United States rose considerably during the New Deal years, reaching a total of nine million by 1940. For the CIO in particular, the gains made as a result of Section 7(a) and the Wagner Act were attributed to the Roosevelt administration.[7]

One striking omission from the Second Hundred Days was any overall industrial or business policy to replace the NIRA. Instead of government planning, the emphasis switched increasingly to the restoration of competition and action against monopoly. One reason for this was that even those New Dealers who favoured government-business co-operation found it impossible to devise a planning mechanism which would not grant so many powers and privileges to business.[8] Farmers were also excluded from the Second Hundred Days. However, when in January 1936 the Supreme Court declared the AAA to be unconstitutional, there was considerable pressure on the Administration from the farmers to do something rapidly to avoid the recurrence of massive overproduction. The answer was the Soil Conservation Act, which, under the guise of conservation, provided financial incentives for farmers to plant fewer soil-depleting crops (which category included most crops in surplus) and more crops which would help to conserve the land. This explicitly addressed the need to raise the income of farmers. Moreover, the creation of the RA prior to the Second Hundred Days was intended to address the problems of poorer farmers for whom the AAA had been more of a problem than a benefit. Indeed, at the time of its foundation there were around 900,000 rural families on the relief rolls.

In terms of political manoeuvring, Roosevelt had successfully diverted the appeal of the demagogues by measures which addressed the needs of the poor, the old and other hitherto marginalized groups. In addition, he struck at the overt concentration and inequities of wealth, themes adopted by both Coughlin and Long. But what had the Second Hundred Days achieved in concrete terms? The gains were considerable, but we need to appreciate the limitations as well as the achievements. The most mixed of the measures passed was probably the Social Security Act. In many ways, it was a revolutionary step; for the first time, the federal government had accepted the thesis that the national government had a responsibility for the individual welfare of all Americans. The Social Security Act provided nation-wide (if not always nationally administered) schemes of old age and employment insurance, and old age assistance of the needy. In addition, provision was made for extra assistance to be given to other groups in need, including the blind, the handicapped and mothers with dependent children, although these categories were to be administered by the states with federal financial assistance.

Yet, important though this principle was, the fact none the less remains that, as William Leuchtenburg has remarked, the act was 'an astonishingly inept and conservative piece of legislation'.[9] It was, first of all, very parsimonious. The first pensions were not scheduled for payment until 1940, and the payment of unemployment benefit was very limited, both in terms of amount paid and the number of weeks for which a claimant was eligible. The omissions were legion. The insurance schemes were funded by employer and employee, with no contribution from the government, and there was no health insurance scheme, as many had hoped. Moreover, at Treasury Secretary Morgenthau's insistence, domestic and agricultural workers were excluded from the act's provisions. Each programme had a separate administrative framework, with differing relationships between federal and state governments. Frances Perkins clearly hoped that some if not all of these problems might be mitigated by further legislation,[10] but this was not to happen. However, whatever the criticisms, and they are many indeed, the act not only provided a valuable start to the provision of a social security state, it also marked an important precedent of principle, the acceptance by the federal government of responsibility for the individual well being of its citizens.

Further weaknesses emerge if we move beyond the Social Security Act itself to consider its place within the overall welfare and relief programmes as envisaged by Roosevelt and his administration. FDR, and indeed Hopkins, had been eager to take the federal government out of the business of direct relief while retaining national responsibility for those hit by the Depression. Hopkins was keen to escape connection with the dole (that is, direct relief) as he believed that 'Give a man a dole and you save his body and destroy his spirit; give him a job and pay him an assured wage, and you save both the body and the spirit.'[11] Hence, FERA was abandoned, receiving its last appropriation in November 1935. In theory, then, there now existed two programmes: one, a work relief programme, aimed at providing temporary, publicly funded jobs for those who were unemployed, the Works Progress Administration (WPA); and the other a social security system tackling the needs of those categories referred to as 'unemployables', most of whom were covered by the provisions of the Social Security Act. The federal government administered the WPA although with local initiative and some local funding, but otherwise played no part in the business of relief. Hence, any 'employables' not offered jobs with the WPA had no federal programme to support them, yet were not really covered by the assistance provisions of the Social Security Act. As a result, they were subject to demeaning local relief processes, with widely differing standards of provision and care. This affected millions of Americans, for the WPA could only provide work for about a third of those wanting it. The young were given special support through the popular National Youth Administration, created in 1935 and run by Aubrey Williams, which provided a wide range of programmes, including schemes to help college students work their way through their degrees.

By choosing to look at the First and Second Hundred Days separately, this book might appear to support those historians who use the terms First and Second New Deal. Such a subdivision is very convenient for the historian seeking to chart the immense flood of legislation in the five years or so of the New Deal. However, there is a real danger of over-emphasizing the elements of change and underplaying the continuity between the two periods. The debate as to whether we can distinguish between a first and second New Deal began with Raymond Moley and Rexford Tugwell, both of whom professed to distinguish a second New Deal after mid-1934. Moley believed that, but for the social security measure, the legislative programme of the New Deal was complete by then; further initiatives were taken by Roosevelt for mainly political reasons. Tugwell argued that, while the Government continued after 1934 to accept its role in relief, welfare and public works, it rejected collectivism and moved from enforcement of planning to the use of regulation, acting on the advice of Chief Justice Brandeis. Both clearly felt that there was a distinct change in mood and policy emphasis.[12] Some historians, the best known of whom is Arthur Schlesinger Jr, also adopted the idea of two New Deals. Schlesinger argues that the tenor of the economic legislation included in the First Hundred Days was distinctly different from that contained in the Second Hundred Days; whereas the first told businessmen what to do, the second told them what not to do. In other words, the first phase represented government-business co-operation and planning across the economy, with restraint of trade incorporated within the NRA codes; the second relied upon a restoration of competition and an atmosphere of hostility to trusts.[13]

Another distinction drawn between the two New Deals is the change in advisers as Brandeisians such as Felix Frankfurter, Benjamin Cohen and Thomas Corcoran supplanted Moley and Tugwell who were com-mitted to central economic planning. Cohen and Corcoran had been with the New Deal administration from the beginning, but whereas in 1934 these two gifted and complementary individuals worked often under Moley's direction, by 1935 they operated independently, not only as legislative draftsmen but also as lobbyists and advisers. Other distinc-tions between the two phases include the switch from an emphasis on relief and recovery to the drive for reform; the transition from the broker state approach resting upon a coalition of different interest groups to a class-based rhetoric; and the increased emphasis upon a strong admin-istrative state and an interventionist executive.[14] In many ways, however, what is at issue is more a matter of emphasis than of substantive change. To suggest that there was a dramatic change in direction within the New Deal in 1935, whether in response to the Supreme Court decision or the growing support for Huey Long, is to overlook the very considerable elements of continuity within the Administration's planning. There was, after all, a matter of only two years between the so-called 'First' New Deal and the 'Second'. In a democratic state, the task of planning and implementing policy is a relatively long-term matter. In many respects, therefore, the difference between the two New Deals was more a matter of presentation than of substance. None the less, in the context of growing threats to the continued New Deal consensus, it is not surprising that the Administration sought to recapture the political initiative, particularly with the next Presidential election a mere fifteen months away. Moreover, as traced at the end of the last chapter, there were a number of popular indications of growing support for more radical change, an articulation of dissatisfaction with the pace and depth of change.

The main change detected between the two New Deals relates to economic policy. It has been suggested that the Administration retreated from an attempt to introduce centralized planning and direction of the economy in favour of an atomistic restoration of competition that actually represented a retrograde, conservative step. Again, however, one should beware of emphasizing too strongly a division into two New Deals in economic policy. The greater emphasis upon the need to police business and restore competition was buttressed by a shift in rhetoric within Roosevelt's own speeches, with a growing emphasis upon class-based appeals and attacks upon 'economic royalists'. However, this was, to a large extent, a response to growing business opposition. Government-business co-operation would only work if both sides were prepared to make compromises. Yet many businessmen, relieved from the immediate worries of total collapse, had begun to resent all curbs upon their freedom of action, as symbolized by the formation of the American Liberty League as a right-wing pressure group.[15] This encouraged Roosevelt in his move away from the broker state to the class-based appeal which dominated the 1936 presidential election. The effect of this, however, was a shift from an emphasis on the control of production to the increase of consumption through more equal access to goods and income. This shift over time is clearly discernible, but it reflected a complex interchange of factors and developments, and cannot simply be located in the three months during the summer of 1935 which comprised the Second Hundred Days.

Even as Congress passed the major legislation of the Second Hundred Days, however, there were signs of two potential threats to the continuity of the New Deal programme which were later to assume growing importance. One is, of course, the hostil ity of the Supreme Court to much of the early New Deal legislation. The Court had adopted a very narrow definition of interstate commerce, and had also raised concerns about the delegation of powers to the President. Despite all the care devoted to drafting legislation, particularly the Social Security Act, it was still possible that the more considered legislation of the Second Hundred Days would fall foul of the Court. Indeed, many employers refused to comply with the Wagner Act, so convinced were they that the measure would eventually be found unconstitutional. In January 1936 the Court found the Agricultural Adjustment Act unconstitutional, arguing that agriculture was not interstate commerce and that Congress could not use its taxation powers to regulate agriculture. As Roosevelt had commented bitterly at the time of the Schechter decision, in its determination to ignore the national nature of the economy and the impossibility of distinguishing interstate from intrastate commerce, the Supreme Court had returned to the 'horse and buggy' era. The Court also demonstrated its general hostility to welfare legislation, even at state level, when in June 1936 it declared that a New York state minimum wage law for women and children was unconstitutional.

The second threat, as yet very minor, was the growing international tension which was to occupy the President, and many in his administration, in the years to come. During the Second Hundred Days another piece of legislation was passed which was the subject of considerable negotiation between the President and Congress – the first Neutrality Act, which became law on 31 August 1935. This Act, which was intended to prevent a recurrence of factors which many Americans believed had led to American entry into the First World War, tied the President's hands in an area where traditionally the executive was in a very strong position, that is, foreign affairs. It allowed the President to proclaim that a state of war existed between countries, at which point he could ban all arms exports to belligerents and warn American citizens of the dangers of travelling on belligerent vessels. At this point, with domestic recovery still the main priority, and with no desire for an active foreign policy, Roosevelt was not necessarily unhappy to have these limitations in place; but over the next four years the scope and compulsion of the Neutrality Acts was to increase substantially, as the threat to international peace also grew.[16]

By mid-1936, the New Deal had still not achieved economic recovery, nor did it appear to have a coherent economic policy. Basic conflicts and anomalies still remained within the administration and there was a clear ambivalence towards the form which economic policy should adopt. However, by then, the New Deal had reached into the lives of millions of Americans in ways that few would have dreamt possible a few years before. This is discussed in more detail in the next chapter. At one basic level, the eight million individuals helped by the WPA, and their families, had good reason to be grateful to the New Deal. However, others were also affected by the WPA; those who used the 100,000 public buildings, 75,000 bridges, 287 airports and the vast network of roads all provided through the WPA, or those who enjoyed less monumental fruits of WPA labour – parks, playgrounds, state guides, slave narratives, library catalogues, murals, paintings and parks. During the 1930s over 45 million people in total (about 35 per cent of the population) received public assistance or social insurance. Whatever the limitations of the New Deal programmes, the fact none the less remains that, compared with most previous administrations, Roosevelt had achieved a tremendous volume of reform in his first term and had fundamentally altered the relationship between the federal government and the American people.

With this reform in place, and with the relief programmes, now spearheaded by the WPA, reaching deeper into the ranks of the needy, and with policies geared to addressing the needs of the farmer as well as the industrial work-force, it came as no surprise that President Roosevelt was re-elected with a resounding majority in the presidential election of 1936, with considerable gains being made by Democrats at all levels. The legion of Roosevelt supporters, increasingly moving into the Democratic party as registered voters in one of the most striking voting realignments of this century, created a strong mass base. This Northern, lower class, urban coalition which swept Roosevelt to a landslide victory – he carried all but two states, Maine and Vermont – proved a permanent part of the Democratic Party, overwhelming its popular base but still leaving the white Southern enclave powerful within the party hierarchy and Congress. The trend towards a populist urban appeal had been set long before 1936, and indeed owed much to the unsuccessful 1928 campaign of Al Smith, but the New Deal years saw the final formation of the coalition. Which groups, then, supported Roosevelt? No doubt many of those who had received relief of some kind, for whom the New Deal had restored hope and some dignity. A Gallup poll in 1936 suggested that FDR received about three-quarters of the lower income votes, 84 per cent of relief recipients and roughly the same proportion of labour union votes.[17] He still retained the support of the farm belt, their endorsement of 1932 given added impetus by the myriad agricultural measures passed by the New Deal. The South was, as ever, solidly Democratic. However, beyond this, we see in 1936 the clear emergence of what is called the new Democratic coalition. Groups, some of them hitherto apolitical, others traditionally Republican in their allegiance, swung behind Roosevelt and, even more significant, remained as part of a solid Democratic coalition throughout the Roosevelt presidency and well beyond.

An important element within this new coalition was organized labour, which, for the first time in an American election, voted as a discernible voting group. The American Federation of Labor (AFL) had tradition-ally refused to lend permanent support to any one party, behaving clas-sically as an interest group, lobbying for its own interests and changing political support according to particular party positions on key issues. However, in April 1936 a number of labour unions, led by United Mine Workers' leader, John Lewis, formed Labor's Non-Partisan League to co-ordinate pro-Roosevelt political activity in the 1936 campaign. In addition, labour provided funds for the Democratic party – over three-quarters of a million dollars. The reasons for this decisive political support lay in the legislation of the New Deal on the one hand, and the new-found assertiveness of American labour on the other. However limited had been Roosevelt's commitment to the cause of organized labour, his re-election was seen as vital. It had, of course, been others, notably Senator Wagner, who had fought to support organized labour's rights to collective bargaining, and employees' rights to decent working conditions, through Section 7(a) and the Wagner Act. However, the New Deal's imprimatur had been crucial. Emboldened by this legislation, labour had in turn seized the initiative and organized in order to support their own interests. The outbreaks of rank-and-file militancy in late 1933 and 1934 gave momentum to the recruitment of workers into the unions. When traditional AFL craft unions failed to respond adequately to the demands of workers in the mass production industries, new and existing industrial unions launched major recruiting drives and, eventually, created their own federation, first in November 1935 as a subshoot of the AFL, the Committee for Industrial Organization, and then, in 1938, as a separate federation. As an increasingly militant, more radical group, organized labour was an important component of the new, more class-based Democratic coalition.

Another important element within the New Deal coalition were the African Americans. Traditionally, those African Americans able to vote (an important caveat)[18] had tended to vote for the party of Lincoln, the Republican Party; there was no indication before 1932 that those living in Northern cities were joining the urban drift into the Democratic fold. By 1936, however, not only were more African Americans, particularly women, registering to vote, but those votes were being cast for the Democrats, the party of Roosevelt. There has been considerable discussion as to why this should be the case, given the association of FDR with key Southern politicians, his refusal to support an anti-lynching bill and the discrimination suffered by many African Americans within New Deal programmes. The answer is straightforward – relief and recognition. However limited and discretionary the relief received by African Americans, it was none the less critical to them, for as a group they had been hit disproportionately hard by the Depression. Similarly, the recognition afforded to the African American population by the New Dealers was constrained by a number of factors, but none the less there were a number of positive signs, such as the appointment of African Americans to senior administrative posts, the end of segregation within government departments and the role played by Eleanor Roosevelt, Harry Hopkins and Harold Ickes in promoting the cause of African Americans. In an important symbolic act, the First Lady met, and was photographed with, African Americans and from 1934 she lent her support to the campaign for an anti-lynching bill.[19] Harold Ickes insisted that the PWA should not neglect the African American community, and the WPA required that there should be no racial discrimination, although such regulations were always difficult to enforce. The number of prominent African Americans employed by the administration rose, led by Mary McLeod Bethune, the head of the Division of Negro Affairs in the National Youth Administration (NYA). Robert Weaver, later to be the first black cabinet member, was employed in the Interior Department and other prominent African Americans were part of an informal 'black cabinet'. The importance of the alphabet agencies to the African American community, and the high regard in which Roosevelt was held, was reflected in many popular songs, including the WPA Blues, the NRA Blues and the FDR Blues. In a song recorded in 1936, entitled, 'Don't Take Away My P.W.A.', blues singer Jimmy Gordon summed it up :

P.W.A., you the best ol' friend I ever seen
Since the job ain't hard and the boss ain't mean'
I went to the polls and I voted, I know I voted the right way,
Now I'm praying to you Mister President, please keep the P.W.A.[20]

All this was in marked contrast to the Republican Party which had begun to follow a lily-white policy in the South.

Also important within the coalition were the many ethnic groups living in the large Northern cities. Irish Americans and Italian Americans had traditionally voted Democratic, but they were now joined by other groups such as the Jews, whose allegiance to the New Deal reached a staggering 90 per cent of those voting. Farmers, too, had benefited during the New Deal, as a combination of New Deal policies and drought conditions had pushed up farm prices steadily during the period. Thus, 1936 saw a critical realignment in party politics in which a major regrouping of traditional allegiances took place. Political scientists have debated as to whether what had occurred was a conversion of previous Republicans or a mobilization of groups which had hitherto not bothered to vote. While the answer is probably a combination of the two, what clearly emerged was the importance of social stratification and class within the realignment. Gerald Gamm has rightly cautioned historians against too simplistic an interpretation of the realignment, for it subsumed a number of different tendencies, but clearly a combination of factors, including the appeal of Al Smith, the Great Depression, the programmes of the New Deal and, eventually, the crisis in Europe forged a new Democratic voting base.[21]

In 1936 the New Deal appeared firmly in place at the fore of the American political scene. By its success in redressing the ills of the capitalist system without destroying it, it had done much to undermine support for more radical parties which might otherwise expect to gain from the hardship of the Depression, notably the Socialist and the Communist parties. Indeed, the political left was virtually wiped out by the New Deal, which diverted and satisfied many of the opposition demands, through its provision of a social security safety net and a 'tamed' union movement. Despite the apparent militancy of labour and agricultural activity, the American people generally were unprepared to abandon the fundamental nature of their capitalist society. This process was assisted by the shift in 1936 of the Communist Party to a popular front strategy, which basically sought the support of liberal and social democratic political movements as part of a battle against what was seen as the greater evil of Fascism. This left the Socialist Party fighting alone against the New Deal, a stand difficult to maintain when the latter appeared to be delivering so much reform. Moreover, the Party sowed the seeds of its own downfall by engaging in internecine feuding. The Socialist Party remained a focal point for a coherent and strong critique of the New Deal, on grounds very similar to those advanced by New Left historians, but did nothing really effective to replace it in power. Thus, surprisingly, opposition from the right remained more powerful than from the left in terms of practical politics, although when it came to an intellectual critique of the New Deal, the left was more effective and vociferous.

Other opponents were also in disarray. The fears of a divided electorate had been undermined by the assassination of Huey Long in September 1935. The Union Party, which sought to bring together supporters of all three main demagogues, had no charismatic leader: Long was dead, Coughlin debarred from standing for office as a Catholic priest. Lacking its most powerful figure, the Union Party, formed by the demagogues to fight the 1936 election, secured less than 2 per cent of the popular vote. On the Right, the vituperative hatred directed by businessmen and the very wealthy at the New Deal[22] failed to conceal the fact that many Republicans found at least some of the New Deal measures appealing. Its 1936 party platform indicated that the party would indeed retain many New Deal initiatives if elected to office, including the national regulation of utilities, payments to the old, soil erosion measures, and federal aid to farmers. The Republican candidate, Governor Alf Landon of Kansas (one of only seven remaining Republican state governors), although a decent man, lacked charisma. Wary of strong central government, he was none the less honest enough to admit his support for some elements of New Deal policy. However, one should not underestimate the strength of opposition from the Right, if only at the level of individual wealthy individuals. Many conservatives were also found in such entrenched centres of power as the Supreme Court (several of whose members bitterly opposed the extension of federal power) and the two houses of Congress. Hidden by the large Democratic majority was the fact that many Democrats, particularly those from the South, were themselves conservatives. There were a number of leading political figures, such as Herbert Hoover and even Al Smith, who advocated conservative ideas fluently and consistently. In the face of opposition from the business community, FDR abandoned attempts to retain an all-class coalition, including business, which had emerged in the First Hundred Days, but which was clearly in disarray by 1935, and instead attacked the group whom he described as 'economic royalists'.

With a strong Democratic coalition behind him, FDR won a landslide victory which excelled his 1932 victory. In an outstanding demonstration of the wide base of his support, he carried all states except Maine and Vermont, while Landon even failed to carry his home state of Kansas.[23] Moreover, this was not simply a personal victory. The Democratic majority in the House of Representatives was 229 and in the Senate 56. The Democratic Party also did exceptionally well at state level, winning state legislatures and governorships which had not been Democratic in living memory. With so massive and sweeping an electoral mandate, with a Congress absolutely dominated by his own party, and with the Democrats also in strong control at state level, Roosevelt entered his second term in an apparently unassailable position, with a clear ideological commitment to a class base very different to that which he had adopted in 1932. For the many New Dealers, in Washington and throughout the country, the election victory appeared both an endorsement of the achievements so far, and a clear signal that further reform was definitely on the political agenda. The way seemed poised for the New Deal to consolidate its role in American politics, continue the reform agenda, and identify a political successor to Roosevelt who could continue the reform impulse after his second term.

Notes

1. The best study of the demagogues, which examines critically the extent to which they posed a radical national threat, may be found in Alan Brinkley, *Voices of Protest: Huey Long, Father Coughlin, and the Great Depression* (Alfred A. Knopf: New York, 1982). As well as the works on Huey Long listed in the Suggestions for Further Reading, see the stimulating essay by Anthony J. Badger, 'Huey Long and the New Deal', in Stephen W. Baskerville and Ralph Willett, *Nothing Else to Fear: New Perspectives on America in the Thirties* (Manchester University Press: Manchester, 1985).

2. It should be remembered that many contemporary commentators assumed that the 1936 election would be a close call. On the concern within the Administration, see James A. Farley, *Jim Farley's Story: The Roosevelt Years* (McGraw-Hill: New York, 1948) p. 51.

3. Message to Congress, 4 January 1935, Rosenman, *Roosevelt Papers*, 4, p. 16.

4. At an early stage in the history of the United States, the Supreme Court had acquired the right to declare that an act should be regarded as null and void because it contravened the terms of the Constitution. As the Constitution was a fairly general

and short document, written in the late eighteenth century, its interpretation was open to changes over time.

5. There are a number of excellent studies by those actually involved in the drafting of the Social Security Act. In addition to those listed in the Suggestions for Further Reading, see also Perkins, *The Roosevelt I Knew*, pp. 278–301; and Thomas H. Eliot, *Recollections of the New Deal: When the People Mattered* (Northeastern University Press: Boston, 1992), pp. 91–144.

6. Mark H. Leff, *The Limits of Symbolic Reform: The New Deal and Taxation, 1933–1939* (Cambridge University Press: Cambridge, 1984), pp. 91–164.

7. There is a rich literature on labour in the New Deal, some of which is listed in the Suggestions for Further Reading. For the Wagner Act in particular, see Joseph J. Huthmacher, *Senator Robert F. Wagner and the Rise of Urban Liberalism* (Atheneum: New York, 1971). See also Gordon, *New Deals*, pp. 204–40.

8. Alan Brinkley, *The End of Reform: New Deal Liberalism in Recession and War* (Alfred A. Knopf: New York, 1995), pp. 40–7.

9. William E. Leuchtenburg, *Franklin D. Roosevelt and the New Deal 1932–1940* (Harper and Row: New York, 1963), p. 132. However, he then went on to point out that it was none the less 'a new landmark in American history'.

10. Perkins, *The Roosevelt I Knew*, pp. 298–9.

11. Quoted in Anthony J. Badger, *The New Deal: The Depression Years, 1933–1940* (Macmillan: London, 1989), p. 201.

12. See Moley, *After Seven Years*, pp. 291–317; and Tugwell, *Democratic Roosevelt*, pp. 326–77.

13. Arthur M. Schlesinger Jr, *The Politics of Upheaval* (Houghton Mifflin: Boston, 1960).

14. On the last point, see Brinkley, *End of Reform*.

15. On this, see George Wolfskill, *The Revolt of the Conservatives: A History of the American Liberty League, 1934–1940* (Houghton Mifflin: Boston, 1962).

16. This book does not discuss foreign policy. Leuchtenburg, *Roosevelt and the New Deal*, locates developments in the New Deal alongside foreign affairs. The most detailed study of foreign policy in the Roosevelt Presidency is Robert Dallek, *Franklin D. Roosevelt and American Foreign Policy, 1932–45* (Oxford University Press: New York, 1979).

17. These figures are given by William E. Leuchtenburg in his excellent study of the 1936 election in 'The Election of 1936', *The FDR Years*, pp. 159–95.

18. Particularly in the South, African Americans were denied the vote through such devices as the literacy test or a requirement that in order to vote one needed to pay the poll tax, which was set at a level beyond the resources of the poorest Southerners (including some whites).

19. Joanna Schneider Zangrando and Robert L. Zangrando, 'ER and Black Civil Rights', in Joan Hoff-Wilson and Marjorie Lightman (eds), *Without Precedent: The Life and Career of Eleanor Roosevelt* (Indiana University Press: Bloomington, 1984), pp. 88–107.

20. Jimmy Gordon, 'Don't Take Away My PWA', quoted in Paul Oliver, *Blues Fell This Morning: Meaning in the Blues* (Cambridge University Press, Canto edition: Cambridge, 1994), p. 36.

21. There is a very useful discussion of the different interpretations of the meaning of the 1936 election in Gerald H. Gamm, *The Making of the New Deal Democrats: Voting Behavior and Realignment in Boston, 1920–1940* (The University of Chicago Press:

Chicago, 1989). See also Sean J. Savage, *Roosevelt: The Party Leader 1932–1945* (University Press of Kentucky: Lexington, 1991), pp. 103–28.

22. For an example of this, see Marquis W. Childs, 'They Hate Roosevelt', *Harpers* (May 1936), pp. 634–42, reprinted in Freidel, *The New Deal and the American People*, pp. 98–104.

23. The scale of this victory was not surpassed until 1984, when Ronald Reagan carried 49 of 50 states. (His opponent, Walter Mondale, at least retained the support of his home state, Minnesota.)

CHAPTER 5

The New Deal in Action

So far, this book has concentrated mainly upon events in Washington. However, recent research makes it easier for historians to appreciate the way in which policies devised in the nation's capital translated into the everyday experience of ordinary Americans throughout the United States. It is the pervasive nature of this experience which, despite the many limitations and failings of the New Deal, won such overwhelming political support for Roosevelt. This chapter examines the methods by which this special relationship with the American people was created. It does so by considering, first, the administration of the New Deal at both federal and state level; second, the explicit determination of the Administration to win public support for its actions and policies; and third, the specific experience of selected groups within the American population. The task of administering the New Deal was a very complex and demanding one. The sheer scale of the legislation and the proliferation of agencies meant that the operation of the federal government was far more fluid than it had been previously, as well as requiring a vastly increased bureaucracy. Much of the legislation was administered, not through existing departments of state, but in new agencies created virtually overnight. The need for skilled staff to operate these agencies led to a massive influx of new administrators into the capital city. To some extent this process was helped by the proviso in some agencies that the posts created under the measures were to be exempt from the Civil Service requirements. As a consequence, recruitment could be a haphazard affair. 'In those early days of the New Deal most people simply knew someone who had confidence in them and hired them.'[1] Even so, the sheer task of providing enough administrators was no light matter. However, as the academic job market plummeted, Washington was a Mecca for the young graduates who flooded into the city and found many opportunities awaiting them. Many of them were young, college-educated (often in law) and exceptionally hard-working and dedicated.

The chance to render public service was one compelling factor in bringing me, and hundreds of young fellows like me, to Washington in 1933. It was as if we were responding, twenty-eight years early, to Jack Kennedy's great challenge: 'Ask not what your country can do for you; ask what you can do for your country'.[2]

An important source of such administrators was Harvard Law School, as Felix Frankfurter directed many of his most promising students, including Benjamin Cohen and Thomas 'Tommy the Cork' Corcoran, to the federal administration. In the later New Deal, 'Tommy the Cork' acted as a guide and mentor to those young protégés, a group known collectively as the Happy Hot Dogs. 'Frankfurter sent me to Tom Corcoran, which was the classic way to get a job in the New Deal.'[3] Within the New Deal, 'outsiders' (women, Jews, Catholics and African Americans) often found opportunities within the bureaucracy.

This was also the age of the expert and the professional. The reliance of Roosevelt upon the Brain Trust during the 1932 election campaign was the first illustration of this. Although it is now commonplace for candidates to draw upon a wide range of opinion, including academics, it was an unusual step at that time. Academics specializing in agriculture, including many social scientists, played an important role in the creation of the AAA. Although FDR was not himself a great economic thinker, the activist policies pursued by his administration enabled different schools of economists to investigate various approaches to the troubled American economy. The Administration was a 'laboratory affording economists an opportunity to make hands-on contact with the world of events'.[4] It also drew upon a wide range of expertise in the drafting of legislation, as is apparent in examining accounts of the formulation of such measures as the NIRA. In another link with academia, Professor Edward Witte of Wisconsin University was the Executive Director of the Cabinet Committee on Economic Security.

However, while the use of expertise and the enrolment of young enthusiasts was a positive step, the federal administration also demonstrated negative features. As the emphasis of the New Deal began to swing more from relief and recovery towards reform, more scope existed for administrators to seek structural changes within the prevailing socio-economic system. Against that, however, the constraints operating against the New Deal, both constitutional and financial, began to come to the fore. It also became apparent that within the New Deal itself were a number of ideological constraints which would not easily be overcome. In addition, a growing number of independent agencies were created, such as the Resettlement Administration. Even the task of ensuring that emergency and permanent bureaucracies worked together, rather than in competition, was an immense, and not always completely successful, one.[5]

Roosevelt was in many ways a shrewd and able administrator. However, to the extent that he kept the reins of power firmly in his own hands, and presided over a massive expansion in the Washington bureaucracy, he also showed certain fundamental weaknesses. In particular, in order to ensure that all real power rested with him, he required Cabinet officers and advisers to consult him before any major decisions were taken. This had the effect of limiting the freedom of action of his key advisers in ways which could be counterproductive. This was particularly the case with what historians have termed his use of 'competitive administration'.[6] This, in effect, meant that FDR balanced power given to one member of his team by rival power given to another. There are a number of examples of this. On a general level, the placing of liberals in the traditional spending departments, such as Interior and Labor, was countered by the appointment of fiscal conservatives to major financial posts. In one department, Agriculture, Roosevelt appointed a liberal as Secretary of Agriculture, Henry Wallace, yet had initially placed the Agricultural Adjustment Administration under his rival, George Peek, a man who believed in government subsidies, uncontrolled production and dumping overseas. In such an atmosphere, other rivalries could soon develop. Agriculture, again, provides a key example. Whereas the liberals in the Legal Department were concerned with the fate of sharecroppers, the traditional Southerners in charge of the Cotton Division of the AAA were determined to retain the old social order and discriminatory practices. A major dispute later developed between Secretary of Agriculture Wallace and Secretary of the Interior Ickes as to the appropriate department in which to base the Forest Service.

The best-known example of competitive administration and the one which required considerable adjudication both by FDR and others, was that between Harold Ickes and Harry Hopkins. There was undoubtedly a personal element within the rivalry. However, the main cause was the disposition of emergency relief appropriations and the priorities assigned, respectively, to public works (under Ickes's direction) and work relief (the responsibility of Hopkins). Although they had some factors in common – both employed workers, both helped stimulate the economy through capital spending – it was work relief which succeeded best in what FDR saw as the main priority, the employment of large numbers of workers from the relief rolls. Public works required more skilled workers in any project and had to devote considerable resources to the provision of materials. The seasonal nature and long lead-in time of the larger projects also weakened their efficacy as a mechanism for relieving want and unemployment. The two men jockeyed for control over the emergency appropriation of five billion dollars in 1935, although in the end an awkward compromise was reached, by which larger projects would come under the remit of the PWA, and smaller ones under the WPA.

Even after the legislation had been passed in Washington, and a bureaucracy created to administer it, much still remained to be done. One difficulty was monitoring the implementation of New Deal schemes. Harry Hopkins adopted the expedient of field administrators, with responsibility for a particular region or group of states, who spent much of their time travelling from locality to locality, checking upon standards. In order to keep track of the extent to which his policies met the needs of Americans, he employed Lorena Hickok, an experienced journalist and friend of Eleanor Roosevelt, as his chief field investigator. Over the first few months of the New Deal, she travelled through much of the United States, reporting on the extent to which relief was reaching the most needy.[7] This precaution was necessary because the use of existing agencies in the states was an important factor in providing a rapid and universal network, yet posed difficulties of central control and direction. FERA began the process of creating a formal partnership between the state governments and federal agencies in an attempt to provide relief across the nation, while acknowledging and respecting the rights of state governments and their superior role (it was assumed) in matters of welfare and relief. State governments were required to create State Emergency Relief Administrations and appoint state directors, as well as providing the matching funds. However, many states had little experience of relief, traditionally relying upon voluntary donations and the localized efforts of the various private charities. They were therefore dependent upon the expertise of professionals from private charities, but also from state-directed organizations. Although some other schemes, notably the CCC and the CWA, were entirely funded by the federal government, it still proved necessary to operate through state agencies. The CCC had a particularly complicated bureaucratic structure, drawing upon expertise from within the Departments of War, Agriculture and the

Interior. The WPA, although a purely federal agency, still relied upon the states to nominate workers, approve projects and provide many of the non-labour costs. However, its introduction still had a dramatic effect on relief spending in some states. In Michigan, for example, once WPA was in place, the cost of relief to the state fell by two-thirds.

The New Deal relied on the state governments to make many of their programmes work. However, each of the 48 states had its own separate government, with its own set of policies, political forces, politicians and electorate. In some instances the states could prove powerful agents of reform. During the progressive period at the turn of the century, it was the states which were the laboratories of reform. However, it was clear that dependence upon states alone could not achieve the total national coverage that was so important if a welfare state was to be introduced. Nor could the economy be revived in a piecemeal fashion. One factor militating against the introduction of health and safety, factory and labour legislation in the past had been the unwillingness of any one state to weaken unilaterally the competitive position of businesses operating within its boundaries. Moreover, most states lacked the resources to implement a comprehensive programme. It was these problems which the New Deal sought to address. However, the fact remained that for constitutional reasons, it was important that the Washington administration should have co-operation from the state governments. A number of schemes relied explicitly upon state co-operation – FERA, WPA, PWA and the social security system, for example. However, many states were slow to take action, trying to use federal funds to balance budgets or meet normal expenses. Even under FERA, which emphasized the importance of state funds, federal money accounted for about 71 per cent of all public and relief spending in 1934–5. Moreover, in many states, at least part of the political structure (either the executive, the legislature, the judiciary or individual politicians) were opposed to the New Deal in some form or other. Local interests were often paramount. Thus, despite the many positive aspects of New Deal state politics, including the dramatic rise in spending on public works, relief and social services, and the widespread acceptance of the federal housing act (by 1937, 42 states had facilitated its administration), farm credit administration and other programmes, we certainly cannot speak of a universal acceptance of the New Deal by the states, even by 1936. The degree of assistance given to individual states by Washington, and the level of co-operation from state administrations, often reflected political orientations rather than economic or social needs.

On the whole, the New Deal failed to produce sustained reform drives at state level, for many of the apparent reform upsurges lasted only a few years at most. Most new state spending was financed by regressive consumer taxes that bore heavily on lower income groups. For a number of reasons, financial, constitutional and political, few states, apart from Georgia, New York, Rhode Island, Wisconsin, Minnesota and Michigan, introduced little New Deals. After 1938, many progressive administrations were voted out of office, before they could do much to implement programmes of reform. There was a new federalism but it was still limited by localist forces at state level. The most rigid conservatism had been undermined, but it was far from gone. The reliance upon the states, although inevitable given the Constitution, was a significant factor in limiting the New Deal's impact. Thus, for example, the federal government provided money for the implementation of the public assistance provisions in the Social Security legislation, but only in proportion to the state funds made available. As a consequence, the level of assistance received by the needy old, the blind and mothers with dependent children varied greatly from state to state.[8]

None the less, the use of the states had a profound effect upon the ways in which the schemes were administered, if only that reliance upon the states too often meant reliance upon state administrators. The New Deal could not hope to appoint from scratch a national network of administrators of the necessary professionalism. While many of those staffing the relief agencies were volunteers, the task of organization and direction had to rest with professionals, which frequently meant the use of existing agencies and programmes. One consequence of this was that in many cases the administrators shared the local prejudices and political leanings. Hence, in the South, there were few relief administrators who believed that African Americans should be awarded relief on an equal basis with whites. Indeed, Lorena Hickok, whose letters generally showed considerable sympathy for those on relief, shared many Southern prejudices, despite the fact that she was a Midwesterner. She commented that under CWA, 'I guess it's the first time in the South that Negroes have ever received the same pay as white men for the same work. And I haven't heard a word of complaint – that is, outright complaint.'[9] CWA, however, was a federally administered project. In other New Deal programmes, such as FERA and the AAA, local prejudices were more

easily satisfied. There were protests that the WPA paid rates so high that
African Americans were no longer willing to pick cotton at the normal
rate. On the other hand, local administrators also understood local needs;
the many small projects handled by the WPA relied upon local know-
ledge to direct them. Yet in some cases, such as the FERA, the social
workers staffing the local administrations felt more in accord with
similarly trained professionals in Washington than they did with local,
elected officials. In short, if many of the programmes were only as good
as the administrators who staffed them, provision was necessarily varied,
and to a large extent the impact of the New Deal upon individual
Americans rested upon such intangibles. The widely diverse opinions of
the WPA's susceptibility to political influence surely reflected the
divergence of the organizers and their own political stance.[10]

Implementation of the New Deal programmes relied not only upon
administrators, but upon the strength of popular support. If the electorate
were in favour of a particular measure, its chances of success were greatly
improved. The effect of the Townsend movement upon Congress is one
example of this. However, it was also necessary that the public should
accept the necessity for increased taxes at state level in order to implement the programmes relying upon state as well as federal funding.
Moreover, a number of other campaigns relied heavily on public support,
such as the hope that Americans would reinforce the NRA campaign by
showing a preference for those companies displaying the Blue Eagle.
Indeed, the very continuance of the New Deal relied upon the electorate
to return pro-New Deal Democrats at the Congressional and Presidential elections. From the beginning of the Administration, therefore, the
task of 'selling' the New Deal to the American people was a very
important one. A significant element in this was the ability of FDR to win
popular support through his speeches, particularly his 'fireside chats'.[11]
The Administration capitalized on his popularity. The President held
twice-weekly press conferences and provided much assistance to the
White House Press Corps. This could not necessarily prevail against the
hostility of press proprietors such as William Randolph Hearst, but it
ensured that details of his initiatives, and of the Administration's views
and goals, reached the American people. Moreover, the level of
assistance provided to the Press Corps ensured the personal sympathy
of many journalists. For example, when the United States came off the
gold standard, a government economist was sent to help the White
House press corps write their reports.[12] Eleanor Roosevelt wrote a

syndicated column, 'My Day', for much of her time in the White House, and that too brought the New Deal more directly into people's minds. Both she and the President were inundated by mail daily, demonstrating that they had succeeded in convincing the American people that they cared about their problems and opinions.[13] Steve Early, the first presidential press secretary, used his links with Paramount to ensure that news of the President was frequently incorporated into the newsreels. However, it was not only at presidential level that attention was given to the presentation of the New Deal. Other Cabinet officers held regular press conferences. Letters received by the President and First Lady were often forwarded to the relevant agencies, which also received their own mail. FERA received around 3,000 letters a day from the two sources. Agencies prepared press handouts and other publicity material to explain their work, drawing upon the pool of unemployed journalists to staff new offices such as the NRA's Division of Press Intelligence. In less than a year, both the NRA and the AAA issued around 5,000 handouts. The Social Security Board prepared a little pamphlet to explain social security in a very straightforward way, which seems to have worked.[14]

The critical factor about the New Deal, however, was that its programmes reached directly into the lives of every American. The many personal recollections collected by Studs Terkel[15] bear witness to the degree to which the New Deal, and its various agencies, permeated the experience of Americans during the 1930s. By the end of the 1930s. those in work (with certain notable exceptions) made contributions to the social security programmes; their hours of work and minimum levels of pay were often dictated by federal legislation. The old, the disabled and single mothers received public assistance under New Deal sponsorship. Millions received relief through a federal agency, or had been given aid with credit. Even an innocuous programme like Rural Electrification affected millions of farm families. It is the vast extent of this direct relationship between the American people and the federal government which will be the focus of the remainder of this chapter. It is clearly impossible to consider every sector of the population. However, we will examine below three important groups; those on relief; the rural population; and women.

In the administration of federal relief, Harry Hopkins in particular believed in the importance of tending a person's self-esteem as well as material need. Where possible, he preferred to see those on the relief rolls receiving work relief rather than a simple dole or a food order. Although the sheer diversity of the FERA, with its heavy reliance on the states, meant that his views could not always prevail, he did all that he could to see that the CWA and the WPA provided appropriate work relief, drawing where possible on the expertise of particular individuals. Even under FERA special programmes were set up to meet the needs of artists, writers, professionals and students. Given the current controversy, particularly in the United States, about the desirability or otherwise of 'workfare', it is important to emphasize that the impact of providing work rather than direct welfare payments was a positive one.[16] Hopkins also set up a special Transient programme, which by its very nature was federal in scope.

The responsibility for work relief after 1935 rested with the WPA. As with the CWA, the WPA paid the prevailing wage, the hours worked being adjusted to ensure that each recipient earned his required budget (thus, skilled workers worked fewer hours than the unskilled). However, no more than one member of a family could be employed and the benefits were still means tested. For those lucky enough to gain WPA placements – in total, about eight million Americans before it was wound up in 1943 – the wages provided on average about twice the relief available under FERA (but only about a quarter of pre-Depression wages), not to mention the undoubted psychological boost of being engaged in work. The work was monotonous for the most part, relied heavily on unskilled construction projects and was designed not to compete with private industry, either in the type of work done or in the wages paid.[17] Even so, there still remain today many concrete testimonies to the work of the WPA, as virtually every community benefited from its construction programmes. As many unemployed craftsmen were available to work on the schemes, and as there was less pressure on the time and number of workers employed on the various schemes, many were of a very high standard (although others, inevitably, consisted mainly of 'made work'). However, the WPA did run into criticisms, some directed towards its innovative professional and creative programmes (the Living Newspaper, for example, fell foul of Congressional opposition) but others towards the charge that it was diverting labour from private business as the rates available challenged private rates. While there is little evidence of a pent-up private demand for labour, there was real anxiety expressed in the South which traditionally had a very low wage economy.

None the less, while many WPA schemes provided unskilled or semi-skilled work, and did little to encourage training, there were a number of examples of more imaginative schemes catering for the particular needs of professional and white-collar workers. Best known are those schemes which catered for the creative arts through the Federal Art Project, the Federal Music Project, the Federal Theatre Project and the Federal Writers' Project. Project workers who later became famous in the creative arts included Orson Welles, Arthur Miller, Richard Wright, John Huston, John Steinbeck and Burt Lancaster. The attitude towards these programmes was ambivalent. In many instances, the intention was to display the positive aspects of American culture and life, with the painstaking collection of historical and geographical data in the state surveys, for example. In the Federal Art Project, the emphasis was upon representational art and the involvement of artists with the community. Its various programmes included the creation of Community Art centres, to provide a free art education for ordinary people, programmes of painting and sculpture in publicly owned buildings such as housing programmes, schools, prisons and hospitals and the Index of American Design which employed graphic artists to produce meticulous representations of American craft design. Art historians are divided on the value of the art thus produced, and at the time some were uneasy about the portrayal of the artist as a wage labourer, but the project represented a significant element in the artists' lives.[18]

While the WPA catered for unemployed urban workers, the New Deal also developed programmes which sought to address the question of rural poverty. The AAA had resisted attempts by the Legal Department to institute a programme of social reform in the South, but the same was not true of FERA, which developed schemes aimed at helping the destitute and low-income rural poor through the Rural Rehabilitation scheme. Although FERA ended in 1935, the work of the Rural Rehabilitation division was absorbed by the newly created Resettlement Administration under the directorship of Rexford Tugwell. This in turn became part of the Farm Security Administration (FSA) formed in 1937 to administer the newly passed Bankhead–Jones Farm Tenancy Act. Together with the Rural Electrification Administration, it did much to improve conditions for poor American farmers. In 1936 the RA set up a Public Health Section to provide medical attention, including hospital and dental care. The rapid spread of electrification, from 11 per cent of all farms in 1935 to a quarter in 1940, improved not only living conditions but farming methods as well. In the Tennessee Valley area, cheap hydro-electric power was provided by the TVA, as well as fertilizer and education in improved farming practices. Elsewhere, farmers were re-settled from submarginal land, farming practices were improved in an attempt to tackle soil erosion and land exhaustion, and credit was made available in order to help tenants buy their own land and purchase livestock and tools. In a number of instances there was an attempt to restructure rural life, with the introduction of some collectives, and the concept of 'grass-roots democracy' in such programmes as the TVA, the AAA and a number of conservation schemes.[19] This assumed that those involved in a scheme should play a part in shaping its administration. It is particularly striking that some of the groups assisted by rural pro-grammes were among the most politically powerless in the United States, a salutary reminder that the New Deal did not simply respond to pressure from powerful interest groups. The FSA also set up camps for migrant workers, often providing free or low cost medical care; the contrast between those camps and the conditions prevailing in the privately-owned camps was graphically illustrated in John Steinbeck's novel, *The Grapes of Wrath*. None the less, the limited appropriations provided considerably reduced the scope of RA activity. It simply could not address the vast problems created as a result of the droughts and subsequent dust-bowl conditions in the Midwest during 1934 and 1935, conditions which ironically contributed to the decline in agricultural production and the subsequent increase in prices.

While genuine attempts were made by the New Deal to assist the poorer farmers, the programmes simply did not do enough to tackle the problem of the rural poor, particularly in the South where poverty was endemic. The reasons for this were legion. In the South, its particular form of tenancy served not only an economic but also a political and social purpose. The Democratic Party was too reliant upon support from white Southerners to consider any serious challenge to the prevailing socio-economic structure. Moreover, lack of funds was a serious handicap. The RA and FSA had hoped to remove 500,000 families from sub-marginal land and to build 50 new towns to help house them. In the event, they relocated only 4,441 families and built three greenbelt towns.[20] There was also an underlying ideological problem, for many of those involved in formulating the New Deal's rural policies still thought in terms of small family farms, owned by those who farmed the land, while others preferred to emphasize the need to provide relief to as many as possible. Tugwell's advocacy of co-operatives fell on deaf ears; even those who were resettled in new communities often thought in terms of ultimately achieving a small farm of their own. The FSA offered loans to enable the purchase of land and livestock, but since prudence dictated that help should only be given to those likely to be able to repay, the most destitute sharecroppers were automatically excluded. Through the work of the FSA Photography Unit, through the reports on rural poverty, the New Deal did much to educate the American public in the conditions prevailing in the most backward areas of the country, and for some families, substantial progress towards a better life was made. But apart from some of the limited initiatives discussed above, there was no serious attempt to tackle the structural problems underlying rural poverty.

The third group we shall concentrate on is that of women. The attitude of the Roosevelt administration was a mixed one. On the one hand, throughout the 1930s the idea was widespread that women, whatever their responsibilities, should not be working if men required their jobs. New Deal legislation and relief programmes accepted the notion that women should be paid a lower rate for the job and did little to address their specific problems. Relief schemes were aimed mainly at the provision of support for families, and thus there was a concentration upon the provision of relief to men. However, there were many women who clearly required relief, including single women dependent upon their own resources, women whose husbands were unable to meet the financial needs of the family and women with dependent children. It is estimated that in May 1934 about a fifth of all urban relief families had a female head and 45 per cent of the unemployables on relief in the cities in 1934 were lone mothers with children.[21] Yet women in this last group, who had received relief from a majority of states prior to the Depression, found their relief needs squeezed by the extraordinary demand from other reliefers after 1929. The First Lady, Eleanor Roosevelt, tried to draw attention to the needs of women by calling a White House Conference on the Emergency Needs of Women in November 1933. She encouraged women to write to her about their problems, and launched all-women press conferences for female journalists. Meanwhile, in September 1933, FERA set up a special Women's Division under Ellen Woodward, who also filled the same role in CWA and WPA, as well as assuming responsibility for professional divisions of WPA. Every state relief director was instructed to appoint a woman to take charge of women's projects, although some did not comply. At one level, the relief agencies did poorly by women, for the proportion of female relief 'places' never approximated their share of those employed or on relief. None the less, the needs of women were not overlooked and special projects were created, often also based on work relief (with the needle replacing the shovel). Women also benefited from the special programmes set up under all three of the main relief agencies to provide work relief for the skilled and professional worker. In many cases, this also benefited the community, by providing education and medical care and advice.

Unfortunately, in the later New Deal, Congress singled out women's projects for curtailment. The provision of mothers' aid assistance under the Social Security Act seemed a positive step, but the vast majority of states already had such schemes in place. Moreover, reliance on state funding as a prerequisite for federal money meant that many such women were worse off under social security than they were under WPA, which they were forced to leave.[22] Moreover, the treatment of the different schemes incorporated under the Social Security Act showed changing attitudes towards women. The only federally-administered programme was the contributory retirement insurance, while unemployment insurance had to take a form approved by the federal government. Both these schemes, with their emphasis on insurance across a working life, came to be associated with the upper-working-class and middle class. Because individual workers contributed from their pay packet, they were seen as an entitlement. However, public assistance schemes, including Aid to Dependent Children, were administered by the states, with subsidies from the federal government and were regarded as subordinate to the insurance provision.[23]

It is noticeable that there was no sustained lobbying by women's groups during the New Deal. Although some organizations continued to press for enhanced protective legislation for women and children, others threw their support behind the Equal Rights Amendment and campaigned against any special legislation.[24] However, gains were made in the political sphere. The Democratic Party decided in 1932 to set up the Women's Division of the Democratic National Committee on a full-time year-round basis under Molly Dewson, and the Party efficiently organized and utilized women in the 1936 Presidential campaign. The Democratic Party convention in 1936 had 219 female delegates, whereas the Republican convention had only 60. The Women's Division produced and distributed 90 per cent of the Democratic National Committee's campaign material. Moreover, the number of women employed in the higher ranks of the federal government increased, and these women regarded themselves as a definite network. As is so often the case in examining the New Deal's consequences, the picture is a mixed one, in which significant achievements were as much coincidental as intentional. The needs of women were recognized in part through the women's network. Relief was given, but not in proportion to need. There are strong parallels between the situation of women under the New Deal and that of African Americans.

We can see, therefore, that the problems of administering the New Deal were many: competitive administration in Washington DC, the problems of staffing new programmes with reliable individuals likely to support and implement the main thrust of the proposals, the difficulties of matching funding and state co-operation, to name but a few. We have already seen in the last chapter how problems arose in the administration of both agriculture and industrial recovery. Staffing from scratch a massive federal programme – or, rather, range of programmes – was, quite simply, impossible, and to some extent the success or failure of the various initiatives reflected the efficacy of existing administrative structures, or the ability to draw upon existing expertise. A mixed picture also emerges when one considers other aspects of the New Deal. Relief, as can be seen, was subject to rivalries in Washington, but also to local prejudices and assumptions. Many of those administering relief had already worked with charities where a distinction had been made between the deserving and the undeserving poor. Others could not comprehend a system where African Americans, or women, should receive the same as white males. Moreover, some schemes suffered from a lack of funds, not least because of the difficulties of persuading the states to contribute fully. The most successful and popular programmes were those funded entirely by the federal government, such as the CCC and the CWA. This, however, merely increased the pressure upon the federal budget. What is clear, however, is that whatever the problems and obstacles, by the time of the 1936 election the New Deal had constructed a nation-wide administration, which brought the federal government into direct contact with the people.

Notes

1. Recollection by Elizabeth Wickenden in Katie Louchheim (ed.), *The Making of the New Deal: The Insiders Speak* (Harvard University Press: Cambridge, Mass., 1983), p. 178. In this interesting collection of reminiscences by the 'second rank' administrators of the New Deal, many of them young graduates from law school, Katie Louchheim captures the sense of excitement, dedication and hard work which permeated the new agencies in Washington DC.

2. Thomas H. Eliot, *Recollections of the New Deal: When the People Mattered* (Northeastern University Press: Boston, 1992), p. 5.

3. Recollection by Thomas I. Emerson in Louchheim, *Insiders Speak*, p. 206.

4. Barber, *Designs within Disorder*, p. 2. On the role of agricultural experts, see Richard S. Kirkendall, *Social Scientists and Farm Politics in the Age of Roosevelt* (University of Missouri Press: Columbia, 1966).

5. An obvious example of this, discussed in more detail below, is the relationship between the Department of Agriculture on the one hand, and the AAA and the RA on the other.

6. A helpful survey of this may be found in William D. Reeves, 'PWA and Competitive Administration in the New Deal', *Journal of American History* 60 (1973), pp. 357–72.

7. A collection of her reports to Hopkins is published as Richard Lowitt and Maurine Beasley (eds), *One Third of a Nation: Lorena Hickok Reports on the Great Depression* (University of Illinois Press: Urbana, 1983).

8. A useful selection of case studies are collected together in John A. Braeman, Robert H. Bremner and David Brody (eds), *The New Deal, vol. II: The State and Local Levels* (Ohio State University Press: Columbus, 1975).

9. Lorena Hickok to Harry Hopkins, 14 January 1934, in Lowitt and Beasley, *One Third of a Nation*, p. 147.

10. Margaret C. Bristol, 'Personal recollections of Assignees to WPA in Chicago', *Social Service Review* (March 1938), pp. 84–7, reprinted in Freidel, *New Deal and the American People*, pp. 20–3.

11. These were used only occasionally, to ensure maximum effect. In the first eight years of his Presidency, Roosevelt gave only sixteen fireside chats. On publicity more generally, see Betty Houchin Winfield, *FDR and the News Media* (University of Illinois Press: Chicago, 1990).

12. Recollections by Richard Lee Strout and Kenneth Crawford in Louchheim, *The Insiders Speak*, pp. 12–19.

13. Roosevelt received 450,000 letters in the first seven days of his Presidency, and thereafter they averaged 8,000 per day.

14. Gertrude Springer, 'So We Told 'em Plain Facts', *Survey* (April 1937), pp. 106–7, reprinted in Freidel, *New Deal and the American People*, pp. 84–90.

15. Terkel, *Hard Times*.

16. W. W. Bremner, 'Along the "American Way": The New Deal's Work Relief Programs for the Unemployed', *Journal of American History* 62 (1975–6), pp. 636–51.

17. Nor did the programmes provide training to attack structural unemployment. Richard Jensen, 'The causes and cures of the Great Depression', *Journal of Interdisciplinary History* 19 (1989), pp. 553–83.

18. Jonathan Harris, *Federal Art and National Culture: The Politics of Identity in New Deal America* (Cambridge University Press: Cambridge, 1995).

19. The TVA is the best-known example of grass-roots democracy. See Philip Selznick, *TVA and the Grass Roots: A Study in the Sociology of Formal Organization* (University of California Press: Berkeley, 1949).

20. These were the rather prosaically named Greenbelt (Maryland), Greenville (Ohio) and Greendale (Wisconsin). The best study of the FSA is Sidney Baldwin, *Poverty and Politics: The Rise and Decline of the Farm Security Administration* (University of North Carolina Press: Chapel Hill, 1968).

21. Linda Gordon, *Pitied But Not Entitled: Single Mothers and the History of Welfare 1890–1935* (The Free Press, Macmillan: New York, 1994), pp. 191–3.
22. Hoff-Wilson and Lightman, *Without Precedent*, pp. 149–50.
23. Skocpol, *Protecting Soldiers and Mothers*; and Gordon, *Pitied but not Entitled*.
24. Susan D. Becker, *The Origins of the Equal Rights Amendment: American Feminism between the Wars* (Greenwood Press: Westport, Connecticut, 1987).

CHAPTER 6

The New Deal in Decline

The election victory of 1936 demonstrated the extent to which the New Deal had, in only four years, impressed itself upon the American people. Although some groups within society – notably, and ironically, the businessmen who had benefited so much from the New Deal – disliked Roosevelt with a vehemence bordering on hatred, the President, as he himself had said in the election campaign, welcomed their hatred. The immense popularity of the New Deal was, of course, a product of the entire two terms commonly associated with the reform programme, while FDR's standing drew also upon his four years as war leader. However, the most obvious and overwhelming expression of the popular success of the New Deal came in the 1936 election. Roosevelt carried on his coat tails Democratic victories at both Congressional and state level. His Cabinet team was experienced, with a number of notable long-term reforms to its credit. The election victory of 1936 not only gave an unequivocal mandate for the continuation of the New Deal reforms of 1934 and 1935, it also re-elected a Democratic Congress to work with the President. It may therefore seem a contradiction to entitle this chapter 'The New Deal in Decline', when it commences at the point where the Roosevelt administration seemed to be at the peak of its popularity and electoral strength. However, the next two years were to see a dramatic shift in the impetus and success of the New Deal. It is important not to overemphasize this point. The WPA and PWA continued with their projects, reaching virtually every corner of the vast United States; the Social Security legislation began to incorporate federal concern for the welfare of its citizens into the permanent polity; through a host of programmes, such as the FSA, the REA and the TVA, the New Deal affected the lives of millions of Americans. New Dealers, at both local level and in Washington DC, continued to work enthusiastically for causes in which they believed; but much of what was achieved in the second term amounted to the continuation and consolidation of the achievements of the first term, rather than the recasting of the reform agenda. New initiatives were fewer on the ground, took longer to pass through Congress, and were frequently rendered less effective by limited appropriations. This chapter will explore why this was so.

The first point to make is that, if the New Deal appeared to lose momentum in the first two years after the 1936 victory, this was not because all the problems facing the United States had been solved. Economic recovery still remained a dream rather than a reality. The 1936 election had been won despite economic performance, rather than because of it. Many social problems also remained, and if liberal thought in the United States had not yet recognized the importance of some of those problems, such as racial discrimination, the Administration acknowledged the existence of economic inequality. In his Second Inaugural in January 1937, Roosevelt identified the need to take action on behalf of the underprivileged 'one third of a nation, ill-housed, ill-clad, ill-nourished' and referred to tens of millions of Americans who were denied 'the greater part of what the very lowest standards of today call the necessities of life'.[1] However, there remained a number of obstacles to the successful implementation of that reform agenda, two major ones being within the constitutional and political framework of the federal government. First, the Supreme Court's Republican majority might decimate the New Deal programme even further in the future. The sheer scale of the 1936 electoral victory had demonstrated that the Justices' interpretation of the Constitution and the proper powers of the federal government was at odds with that of the American public. However, as a non-elected body, the Supreme Court was meant to be aloof from popular opinion and pressure. Second, as well as the judicial aspect of government, the New Dealers were also increasingly conscious of another problem: the proper administration and planning of the executive branch of government. In order to maintain an overview of the economy, initiate legislation and exercise the prerogatives which had been expanded through New Deal legislation, as well as co-ordinate the work of the multiplying alphabet agencies, the Roosevelt administration was convinced that a proper executive structure was required. Thus, the continuation of reform and the proper implementation of the powers already given to the President required a more efficient executive branch and a co-operative judiciary. However, neither of these issues had been discussed during the election campaign and as a consequence, the Administration could not claim an electoral mandate for action. In seeking to reform the Supreme Court and extend the power of the executive, Roosevelt succeeded only in antagonizing Congress, which increasingly turned against him. Meanwhile, the newly Democratic administrations in many states disappeared within two years.[2] As the second term continued, the assumption that Roosevelt would retire from office in 1940, in accordance with the hallowed two-term tradition, reduced his powers of patronage. It is in this broader context, while still remembering the continuing work of New Deal agencies throughout the United States, that we need to consider the second term.

FDR and his administration were well aware that all their work might yet be undone by the Supreme Court. Prior to the 1936 election, the President had discussed a number of options with his Cabinet and other advisers, such as Professor Felix Frankfurter of Harvard University. The options included a constitutional amendment removing the Court's right to declare a piece of legislation unconstitutional.[3] Roosevelt eventually decided to wait until after the election campaign but, as a consequence, he could claim no mandate for his determination to address the judicial problem as a matter of the highest priority. None the less, he was determined to check the Court's powers and address its innate conservatism. In his State of the Union message in January 1937, the President criticized the judicial branch for failing to meet the demands of democracy. On 5 February he sent a message to Congress asking for judicial reform, thus signalling that this, rather than further social reform, was the first priority of his second term.

It is not my intention to discuss the Supreme Court battle in any detail, as this is in many ways more appropriate to a biography of FDR than a history of the New Deal. This reflects the manner in which the President approached the issue. Although in formulating the eventual bill he worked very closely with his Attorney General, Homer Cummings, he otherwise took little counsel.[4] The Cabinet and Congressional leaders were informed – not consulted – on the day that the message requesting the legislation was sent to Congress. With a measure as sensitive as this, which addressed the very Constitution itself, such a failure to elicit and build support reflected poor political judgement. Moreover, the proposal was itself flawed. The bill provided the President with the power to appoint an additional judge to a federal court (including the Supreme Court) should an existing judge who had served at least ten years fail to retire within six months of his seventieth birthday. In all, he could appoint up to six additional judges to the Supreme Court and a further 44 to lower federal courts. This, however, would do nothing to address the reason given by FDR for the measure, that is, the slowness of the Court in deciding important cases, as in such cases the Court sat in its entirety. The measure met with considerable opposition, led by Senator Burton Wheeler, an erstwhile Roosevelt supporter.[5] Despite the unceasing efforts of the Senate Majority Leader, Joe Robinson, it occupied most of the first session of the new Congress, destroyed much of Roosevelt's popular support and allowed the effective mobilization of conservative opposition – all to no avail. The Court packing plan, already on weak ground since it was based upon specious reasoning, was destroyed absolutely by the famous 'switch in time which saved nine'. In April and May 1937 the Supreme Court declared that a number of New Deal measures, including the Wagner and Social Security Acts, were constitutional. This change of heart reinforced Congressional opposition, and the eventual Judicial Procedure Reform Act made only minor and cosmetic changes to the federal judiciary.[6]

Opinion differs among historians as to whether the 'defeat' was in fact victory, since ultimately Roosevelt secured the constitutionality of his key measures and the chance to appoint a number of his own men to the Supreme Court, commencing in May 1937 when the conservative Justice Van Devanter resigned.[7] Thus, the New Deal gained in that the key measures of the Second Hundred Days, which incorporated long term reform, were declared constitutional, while the Court's new willingness to contemplate labour laws on wages and hours encouraged the development of the Fair Labor Standards Act. However, those gains had been made at great cost. First, the fears aroused by the President's desire to tinker with the Constitution produced a backlash against plans for executive reorganization; the creation of an effective White House administration had to await another President. Second, the Court fight had starkly revealed a structural problem within the Democratic Party; its uneasy coalition of white Southern conservatives and a working-class, ethnic, constituency in the Northern cities. This split was too fundamental to be easily papered over, once it came to the fore, and the development of opposition to the Court plan emboldened many Southern conservatives in Congress who had hitherto hesitated to challenge a President whose position seemed invincible. Once created, the conservative coalition of Southern Democrats and Republicans did not disappear and continued to hamper the New Deal through its opposition to 'radical' schemes and its unwillingness to appropriate sufficient funds to support New Deal projects. Moreover, the important psychological opportunity for future reform, the first Congressional session after sweeping electoral victory, had been dissipated. Without wishing in any way to downplay the significance of business hostility and the impact of the Roosevelt recession, it seems clear that the waste of the critical first Congressional session allowed new problems to build up, making the restoration of a reform spirit impossible. In the succeeding years, apart from the Fair Labor Standards Act and the Soil Conservation Act, most of the measures passed were either minor in intent, or deprived of any real effectiveness by a lack of funds, as was the case with the Farm Tenancy Act and the National Housing Act. It is difficult to avoid the conclusion that Roosevelt's political misjudgement had serious consequences for the reform impulse of the New Deal.

Other factors contributed to the growing resistance within Congress. Some New Dealers continued to place great emphasis upon the need for executive reorganization and a strong Presidency, thus simply exacerbating Congressional opinion. Within the country at large, there was growing opposition among businessmen to the New Deal in general and to the President in particular. The demise of ideas of government-business planning, the legislation of the Second Hundred Days and the rhetoric of the 1936 election campaign (which, admittedly, targeted big business and economic royalists rather than businessmen across the board) had already caused alarm. The support given by the New Deal to organized labour during the NRA and in the Wagner Act caused consternation among businessmen. The fear that the balance had swung too far towards labour was reinforced by the wave of labour militancy in early 1937. This was at a time when most employers believed that the Wagner Act would be found unconstitutional, and hence the more belligerent opponents of unionization, in the automobile and steel industries in particular, continued to resist effective collective bargaining. In response, unions turned to a new device, the sit-down strike, first used successfully at the Akron plant of the Goodyear Rubber Company in August 1936. By occupying factories, workers prevented the employment of strike breakers and halted production. Many conservatives believed that this was a result of the support and encouragement given to the labour force by the federal government. Others were perturbed that Roosevelt did nothing to seize the initiative by sending in the troops to restore ownership.

In fact, FDR had never been a positive supporter of organized labour.

While the refusal of the Administration to support the employers whole-heartedly played its part in the events of 1936–37, it is important to recognize the strength of rank-and-file militancy, mobilized by the new and more effective unions of the CIO. It was because of the upturn in the economy at this time, rather than because of a change in philosophy, that a number of companies were forced to accede to union demands for recognition.[8] Between February and April 1937 General Motors, US Steel and Chrysler all accepted union representation. Although this clearly represented a victory for organized labour, it further strengthened conservative and business opposition to the New Deal. Again, ironically, the consequences were very different from those anticipated at the time. To the benefit of many employers, the Wagner Act introduced a more advanced phase in labour relations, with the incorporation of unions into a contractual relationship, in which they helped to enforce industrial peace. Moreover, this, together with the later Fair Labor Standards Act, actually benefited employers in labour-intensive industries, as the enforcement of minimum standards on wages and hours prevented more enlightened employers from being undercut by very low wage production from areas such as the South.

The major obstacle to further reform, however, came from within the Administration itself. For all the financial and currency experiments, and the planning of the NRA and the AAA, the New Deal had never suc-ceeded in solving the country's economic problems. Planned scarcity had effectively failed, even before the Supreme Court had delivered the death blow to the NRA. There had always been an uneasy tension between the advocates of deficit spending, such as Hopkins and Ickes, on the one hand, and the fiscal conservatives, led by Secretary of the Treasury Morgenthau, on the other, over the extent of deficit spending in order to fund New Deal programmes. Although there had been considerable improvement from the dark days of 1933, unemployment continued to exceed seven million and there were few signs of returning business confidence in terms of increased levels of spending and investment. Despite this, however, the Treasury argued strongly that the time had come to test the confidence of private investment by cutting government spending, an argument which the President accepted. FDR tended by inclination to be on the side of caution and he still aspired after a balanced budget. In June 1937, he cut government spending, particularly on WPA and PWA. This was based upon hopes that the economic recovery experienced over the last two years represented a return of business confidence, and hence government spending would be replaced by private investment and production. However, for a combination of factors, no doubt including business dislike of New Deal policies and labour militancy, the required private investment simply was not forthcoming in sufficient amounts. Meanwhile, the economy was simultaneously affected by the first collection of the social security taxes. This amounted to a very rapid reversal of the trend in government spending, for in 1936 a one-off payment of veterans' bonuses, amounting to $1.4 billion, had greatly stimulated the economy. The net result was a sharp downturn in the economy, soon known as the Roosevelt recession. The Federal Reserve's index of industrial production fell by more than a third between August 1937 and May 1938. On 19 October 1937 stock prices collapsed and within a short time unemployment reached ten million again.[9] The downturn was in some ways more dramatic than that of 1929. After four years of the New Deal, Roosevelt could not easily escape the blame for the economic problems.

Rather than planning for long-term reform, the Roosevelt administration had to return to the task of restoring the economy as rapidly as possible. Even so, opinion differed as to the best strategy to follow, and for some time Morgenthau's belief that the economy had to be left to its own devices prevailed. In essence, this represented an important turning point in the New Deal: would those who believed strongly in reform, and who had done so much to shape the New Deal prevail, or would FDR return to the path of a fiscal conservative? Eventually the President accepted the prompting of the spenders within the administration, notably Ickes, Hopkins and Marriner Eccles (Chairman of the Board of Governors of the Federal Reserve). In April 1938 he steered through Congress a massive $3.75 billion spending programme, financed by deficit spending. Public spending on relief and public works, rather than the price-fixing which had distinguished the Administration's response to depression in 1933, represented acceptance of a new interpretation of economic recovery. Instead of reducing production, the Administration increased consumption through anti-trust measures and, above all, the improvement of spending power through labour and welfare legislation.[10] Even so, the President was at pains to stress that his policy was 'following tradition as well as necessity', emphasizing that one goal was 'to help our system of private enterprise to function'.[11]

Although Roosevelt had little difficulty in securing an appropriation so close to the 1938 mid-term elections, during 1937–38 Congress was reluctant to adopt other major legislation. In 1937, it passed the Bankhead–Jones Farm Tenancy Act and also the Wagner–Steagall Housing Act which created a United States Housing Authority to promote slum clearance and the construction of affordable housing. However, the impact of this measure was limited by an appropriation of only $500 million, with no more than 10 per cent to be spent in any one state. Moreover, Congress had failed to enact the 'seven little TVAs',[12] while the Fair Labor Standards Bill, which regulated wages and hours, had stalled in the House of Representatives. FDR called Congress into special session in October 1937 to address the problems of the slump, but little concrete action was forthcoming until February 1938 when the second Agricultural Adjustment Act enabled the Commodity Credit Corporation to store crop surpluses and make loans against the collateral of the crops in order to shore up agricultural prices. It took until June 1938 for the Fair Labor Standards Act to be approved, although the President had made a public appeal for its acceptance on 30 April. Congress may have voted a massive appropriation for relief in April, but in May it passed a Revenue Act which cut corporation tax in a bid to stimulate private investment. The first eighteen months of the second term had therefore been sparse in terms of reform legislation, with a recalcitrant Congress blocking many of the Administration's requests. The business community showed no sign of renewed confidence in the American economy and the weaknesses in the New Deal's economic policies were graphically illustrated in the Roosevelt recession.

If the New Deal were to regain the political initiative, positive action was required. However, as a direct result of the Court fight, it had lost the support of many conservative Democrats whose opposition in Congress thwarted many of the hopes and goals of the reformers within the administration. This reflects the difficulties which the New Dealers faced in seeking to control the Democratic Party. In its electoral base, the party was emerging as a predominantly urban based, liberal coalition, but within the party hierarchy, and particularly within Congress, Southern rural conservatives retained control. They had the support of the Vice President, John Nance Garner, and control of many important Congressional committees. Their preference for balanced budgets, states' rights and limited government was the very antithesis of all that the New Deal had accomplished so far. Lulled into a false sense of superiority by the honeymoon of the first term, Roosevelt still expected to exercise control over Congress; but as his second term continued, that became more difficult.

This growing opposition to FDR, and the New Deal generally, by conservatives within the Democratic party was intensified after 1938, when Roosevelt tried, unsuccessfully, to rid the party of some of his critics. In the early summer of 1938 he decided to intervene in the Congressional elections, making it plain that he would support only pro-New Deal Democrats. He particularly targeted the primaries held within the party at state level to determine the Democratic nominee for office – usually at Senatorial level. Roosevelt hoped to secure a Democratic Party that was clearly progressive, enabling it to appeal to liberal Republicans and establish a massive new electoral coalition. However, it was against tradition for the President to intervene in local primary elections, and by so doing he created resentment rather than support.[13] The result was that in the mid-term elections, the Republicans made sizeable gains and Roosevelt's intended Democratic targets enjoyed electoral success, thus simply strengthening the position of the conservatives within the Democratic Party.

Meanwhile, the popular impetus behind the New Deal, which might have exerted public pressure upon recalcitrant Congressmen and senators, was much reduced by economic recession and labour unrest. Coinciding with this came the new interest in foreign affairs where Roosevelt's policies were not universally popular, particularly in Congress. From 1937 onwards, the time was inauspicious for further large instalments of reform and Roosevelt diverted more of his attention to foreign affairs. Acts were, of course, passed in the next two years, as the Chronology shows, but they were minor in extent compared to the first term and had often to be moderated before Congressional approval could be obtained. Meanwhile, the implementation of many existing programmes was hindered by reductions of spending in 1937, while the rapid build-up of opposition was reinforced by developments at local level as state administrations became more conservative.

Thus, for a number of reasons, the reform impetus of the New Deal slowed after 1937. Despite that, there were some gains of a permanent nature during 1937–38. The new agricultural act of 1938, while seeking to retain some of the elements of the old AAA, introduced to American farming the concept of an 'ever normal granary'. Under this programme, surplus stocks of key commodities would be held in storage until the next year in order to avoid downwards pressure on prices; farmers would be encouraged to participate by price-support loans, offered on the stored crops. If the price fell, the Commodity Credit Corporation would retain the crop, cancelling the debt. This was intended to address the wide fluctuations between years of good and bad harvests which the natural disasters of the 1930s had aggravated. This concept continued to underpin American agricultural policy into the 1960s and contributed to the steady increase in farmers' purchasing power during the New Deal years, until such time as wartime demand once again brought prosperity to the American farmer. The Fair Labor Standards Act passed in June 1938 incorporated permanently the gains on maximum hours, minimum wages and working conditions first accomplished by the NRA. Although, in common with many New Deal measures, it excluded farm workers and domestic servants, and did not fully cover all non-farm workers, this measure introduced for the first time the notion of a national minimum wage (25 cents per hour) and a maximum working week (44 hours). It also banned from interstate commerce any goods manufactured, even in part, by children under the age of sixteen. At a less dramatic level, there were some extensions to the Social Security Act, including the extension of pension coverage to widows and dependants, and more funds for the WPA. April 1939 saw the passing of the Administrative Reorganization Act which allowed the regrouping of agencies under umbrella offices such as the Federal Security Agency, Federal Works Agency and the Federal Loan Agency, and also allowed an expansion in the executive office of the President. However, this was a more limited measure than Roosevelt had wished. He had hoped to create two new departments, Welfare and Conservation, improve the President's administrative support and provide for a more wide-ranging rationalization of agencies and bureaux.

After 1937, the main thrust of economic policy was a continuation of FDR's campaign against the economic royalists, notably through the creation in June 1938 of a joint legislative-executive Temporary National Economic Committee (TNEC), established to investigate the concentration of economic powers and the problem of monopolies. This was accompanied by the appointment of Thurman Arnold as chief 'trust-buster', within the anti-trust division of the Department of Justice.[14] These moves reinforced the shift in the New Deal's economic position from a pro-business approach centred on planning and production control to an attack on restrictive price fixing and the stimulation of consumption. The move in April 1938 to a policy of deficit spending reinforced this consumptionist approach. The Temporary National Economic Committee hearings were used as a sounding board for the advocacy of increased consumption stimulated by public expenditures. This, coupled with Hopkins's appointment as Secretary of Commerce, strengthened the calls for continued deficit spending, The regulation of business took other forms as well: on 24 June 1938, Congress passed, albeit in a much amended form, the Food, Drug and Cosmetics Act requiring manufacturers to list product ingredients on labels and forbidding misleading advertising.[15]

The goal of economic recovery was still elusive, however. Nor did the Administration apparently have a central, coherent economic programme to offer. Although many in the Administration were moving towards a greater acceptance of Keynesian ideas, this was not universal and did not include the President. The TNEC reinforced the Administration's rhetoric against 'economic royalists', but its work was fairly rapidly overtaken by events. The outbreak of war in Europe during 1939, followed by the rearmament of the United States and its subsequent entry into the war, placed a high premium on business co-operation and saw a return to business self-regulation and close contact between government and industrialists. The priorities of the Administration changed drastically. Harry Hopkins moved from the field of welfare to that of foreign affairs, and reform programmes were overwhelmed by the needs of the wartime economy – as Roosevelt put it, Dr New Deal had been replaced by Dr Win-the-War. This was, perhaps, just as well, as Congress showed clear signs of wishing to restrict the New Deal. In 1939, it cut $150 million from the President's proposed relief appropriation and directed that all WPA workers who had been employed for eighteen consecutive months should be dismissed; in August, over three-quarters of a million had to leave the WPA projects. Moreover, Congress also demonstrated its dislike of the more innovative schemes within the WPA, attacking in particular Federal Project One, which was the collective name for many of the more innovative programmes for art, music, theatre and writing.[16]

In many ways, the end of the New Deal, at least in terms of new legislation and initiatives, was signalled by the State of the Union Address in January 1939, in which for the first time the main focus was on foreign and not domestic affairs. However much this may have suited Roosevelt, as his administration became bogged down and lost its political initiative, it also reflected the worsening international scene in the nine months preceding the outbreak of the Second World War. It may, therefore, seem appropriate to end a study of the New Deal at the end of 1938, or at the very least in 1940, with the end of Roosevelt's second term. Indeed, had all things been equal, FDR was expected to retire from the presidency at the 1940 elections, in keeping with the tradition that no president serve more than two terms. Things were not equal, however. Although Roosevelt did not actively seek the presidency in that he refused to state publicly that he was seeking renomination, his supporters engineered a nomination by declaration, and against all precedent, he stood and won again in 1940. The reasons for this, apart from personal ambition, were twofold. First, there was no obvious New Dealer poised to take over the Democratic nomination from him. Harry Hopkins, one possible contender, had been seriously ill and other known New Dealers all had possible drawbacks. Perkins was a woman, Ickes had come to the New Deal as a Republican, and many other important figures such as Thomas Corcoran had no strong base within the party. Moreover, the party still contained powerful conservative elements, including Roosevelt's Postmaster General, James Farley, who might use the opportunity to return the party to its old ways. The two 'party regulars' most likely to stand for nomination were Farley himself and Vice President Garner, neither of whom were sympathetic to the goals of the New Deal.[17] If Roosevelt wished to protect the New Deal, he had to continue in office himself. The second reason, and the one ostensibly guiding his decision, was the parlous state of foreign affairs. Even though the interregnum was now two months, not four, it was not the right time to leave foreign affairs in the hands of a lame-duck President, nor was it necessarily good for an untried leader to assume responsibility for foreign affairs. For both these reasons, Roosevelt was nominated, and, in November 1940, was re-elected.

This election demonstrated again that, however much it may have run out of steam in the preceding two years, the New Deal was still popular. Although critical of the New Deal in speeches and rhetoric, Republican nominee Wendell Willkie stood on a platform which implicitly accepted much of its legislation. Despite his challenge to the two-term precedent set by no less a figure than George Washington, Roosevelt won a substantial victory, with 27.2 million popular votes and 449 seats in the electoral college. He therefore won over 54 per cent of the popular vote. Although Willkie, with 22.3 million votes, had gathered more popular support than either of his two Republican predecessors, he still carried only a small handful of states, mostly in the grain belt. The success of the New Deal in eliminating the radical threat was demonstrated even more clearly in this election. Norman Thomas the Socialist Party candidate won only just over 100,000 votes, and the Communist contender, Earl Browder, obtained under 50,000. The election results demonstrated the extent to which the New Deal, and the President, had become an accepted part of the American political system.

Although the war did not come to the United States until 7 December 1941, it dominated the last five years of Roosevelt's presidency. It is helpful to pause and reflect on how the wartime experience built on New Deal precedents, and how far it challenged them. The record, as one might expect, is a mixed one. In some quite significant areas, the war brought changes that the New Deal had been unable to secure. In the summer of 1940, Congress passed a massive appropriation for defence spending and, in March 1941, Lend Lease was introduced with an initial appropriation of seven billion dollars. This was used by the United States' future allies to purchase goods in the United States, and by the end of the war $50 billion was spent. The armed forces expanded in the course of the war from 1.6 million in 1941 to 11.4 million by 1945, and, coupled with the increased demand from the civilian labour force, helped address some of the problem of surplus labour. By 1942, the United States had achieved full employment. Thus, with a massive increase in government spending, the subsequent stimulation to the economy brought the elusive recovery which the New Dealers had sought in vain. This was largely due to deficit spending. While the national debt had increased by $27 billion during the period 1930–40, it increased by $215 billion between 1941 and 1945. Moreover, for the first time during the war, the taxation system came into play as an effective means of redistribution of wealth. By the Revenue Act of 21 October 1942, combined corporate income tax was set at 40 per cent, excess profits tax was a punitive 90 per cent and the number of Americans paying federal income tax increased sharply to almost 50 million. War brought the end of sustained domestic reform initiated by the Administration, but it accomplished what the New Deal had been unable to achieve, a return to prosperity and full employment.[18]

Moreover, the Roosevelt administration's commitment to reform, at least rhetorically, remained strong during the war. In government planning and control of the economy, the rights and interests of labour were carefully safeguarded through control of prices and government monitoring of wage limits – for example, in July 1942 the War Labor Board announced a formula for wage levels which effectively gave most American workers a 15 per cent pay increase. Shortly after his re-election, in his State of the Union address in January 1941, Roosevelt employed the concept of the Four Freedoms – freedom of speech and religion, freedom from want and fear – that were to be important slogans in wartime propaganda. In the Atlantic Charter of August 1941 Roosevelt and Churchill agreed that the peoples of the world should be able to enjoy the Four Freedoms. In June 1941 Roosevelt addressed the issue of racial equality, one which he had hitherto ignored, when, by executive order, he required African Americans to be admitted to federal job training programmes, outlawed discrimination in defence contract work and established a Fair Employment Practice Committee. Although this was only done to pre-empt a threatened march of African Americans on Washington, it none the less represented the first recognition of the problem of civil rights, which was to become increasingly important in liberal thought after the war. In October 1944, during the presidential election campaign, Roosevelt called for an economic Bill of Rights, based on large-scale public spending to sustain American prosperity after the war. There were also signs of a more liberal international economic policy when the Bretton Woods conference of July 1944 set up an International Monetary Fund and the International Bank for Reconstruction and Development, and committed the United States to a policy of fixed currency exchanges (based on the dollar and gold) and aid for economies facing difficulties. The continued public support for FDR was clearly demonstrated in the 1944 election when, despite being clearly very ill, he won the election with 25.6 million popular votes and 432 votes in the electoral college.

However, much of the reform agenda remained at the level of rhetoric rather than action. Leaving aside the obvious preoccupation with the war, and the impact of economic recovery and virtually full employment as a result of conscription and wartime production, there are other reasons why this might have been the case. At the end of his second term, Roosevelt had moved towards an economic policy based on anti-business rhetoric, increased taxation and regulation, and a consumptionist emphasis. This hostility was reciprocated by the business community whose vehement dislike, for Roosevelt personally and his administration in general, had been vociferously expressed in the press and in private. However, if the war economy were to function smoothly, it was essential that, in a capitalist society, the state had the co-operation of businessmen who had the necessary expertise. In the Second World War, as in the First, government planning and direction of the economy to meet wartime priorities relied heavily on so-called 'dollar-a-year' men seconded from their normal activities. They played a significant role in new government agencies which exercised sweeping powers of direction over the economy. Even before the United States became a belligerent, in order to meet the needs of Great Britain and, later, the Soviet Union, new agencies were created.

In January 1941, the Office of Production Management was created by executive order, under the joint direction of William Knudsen of General Motors and Sidney Hillman of the CIO. In August, a supplies priorities and allocation board was set up under Donald Nelson of Sears Roebuck. In April, a Roosevelt adviser, Leon Henderson, was appointed to head a new Office of Price Administration and Civilian Supply to protect consumer interests against inflation. The imposition of controls increased once the United States was actually at war. In January 1942, the Emergency Price Control Act empowered the price administrator to set maximum prices and rents in key areas of the war economy. Three months later, in April, the Office of Price Administration issued a general maximum price regulation, fixing many prices and rents at the level of March 1942 for the duration of the war. In the same month, the War Production Board, chaired by Donald Nelson, was given command of the domestic war economy. In October 1942, a new Office of Economic Stabilization was set up under Supreme Court Justice James F. Byrnes, which assumed complete control over the allocation of steel, aluminium and copper and froze agricultural prices.

It is, however, noticeable that, in all the initiatives to control prices and rents, there was no curb on profit levels. Moreover, labour found itself increasingly curtailed. While there was a clear desire to avoid any reduction in standard of living as a consequence of inflation, labour was also prevented from seeking to capitalize upon its new favourable position after ten years of depression. On 12 January 1942, a War Labor Board was created to prevent strikes and reconcile wages with control over inflation and the war economy, and soon developed a group of experienced administrators who continued to be active in labour arbitration after the war. While the Board promised to maintain existing union membership and rights of collective bargaining, new workers would not be compelled to join a union, although they had to 'opt out' within fifteen days.[19] In April 1942, a War Manpower Commission was established to channel and control the flow of workers into the war industries. When, in May 1943, John Lewis called a general coal strike in an attempt to win a pay increase, the President seized the coal mines and ordered the miners back to work. In the emergency situation, no interruption to production could be permitted; this required a more directive attitude towards labour. During the First World War, labour had been appeased by the granting of rights of collective bargaining but having won those rights permanently during the New Deal, there was less justification for a self-denying policy during the Second World War.

The second reason for the lessening of the reform impulse came as a consequence of the mid-term elections of November 1942, in which the Republican Party made considerable gains in Congress. As a result, Congress was now completely dominated by a coalition of Southern Democrats and conservative Republicans, making it virtually impossible to contemplate the smooth passage of reform legislation. From 1939 Congress had acted as a powerful check to the Administration. Now it found itself in a position to challenge the President more directly, and even to take the initiative, secure in its ability to override a presidential veto if necessary. In both 1943 and 1944 the House savaged Roosevelt's proposals for increased taxes, and in 1944, when Roosevelt vetoed the Revenue Act, Congress passed it again over his veto. The same was true of the War Labor Disputes Act of June 1943 which empowered the President to seize any strike-bound plant and made a 30 day cooling off period and secret strike ballots compulsory. Even had the President wanted to introduce further reform – and there are few indications that he did, as he became increasingly involved in the direction of the war, and as the Cabinet became far less active – his chances of pushing legislation, or appropriations, through Congress, were remote.

However, if the New Deal had, as Roosevelt claimed, been replaced by the priority of winning the war, that did not mean that the New Deal agenda was removed from sight. The presidential elections of 1936 and 1940 had demonstrated how strongly entrenched many of the New Deal initiatives had become. If relief was no longer an issue, the Economic Bill of Rights speech suggested that Roosevelt had fully recognized that continued economic recovery relied upon high levels of government spending and executive planning of the economy. By 1940, as Barber demonstrates, economic thought within the administration had evolved towards acceptance of 'a domesticated version of Keynesian-style macroeconomics' based on high consumption and low saving.[20] Although the demands of the war economy necessitated control of private consumption, wartime planning for the post-war world was predicated along those lines. The success of deficit spending during the war also created greater support in the country as a whole for government management of the economy in order to achieve full employment and economic growth. In particular, many businessmen now recognized the important role of government and the significance of mass consumption.

In terms of reform, there remained a number of gaps in the New Deal provision. With the end of the war, however, there was rapid acknowledgement of the need to address these omissions. Franklin Roosevelt died in office, on 12 April 1945, and so was not in the White House to restore the New Deal to the political arena. However, his successor, Harry Truman, was willing to remind the American people of the legacy of the 1930s. Only a few weeks after victory against Japan, on 6 September 1945, Truman used the opportunity of a message to Congress to call for the relaunching of New Deal reform, including the needed expansion of social security, increased minimum wages, more slum clearance, the creation of a system of national health insurance, full employment legislation and the extension of wartime economic controls, with the aim of meeting Roosevelt's aim of an Economic Bill of Rights.[21] This was a clear indication of the extent to which the New Deal had created a strong base in liberal thought. In Truman's Fair Deal, Kennedy's New Frontier and Johnson's Great Society, the reform agenda created by the New Dealers in the 1930s was consolidated and expanded to meet the needs of a prosperous United States.

Notes

1. Second Inaugural, 20 January 1937, Rosenman, *Roosevelt Papers*, 6, pp. 4–5.
2. A thorough picture of the New Deal at state level may be obtained from James T. Patterson, *The New Deal and the States: Federalism in Transition* (Princeton University Press: Princeton, 1969).
3. For contemporary opinions see Max Freedman (ed.), *Roosevelt and Frankfurter: Their Correspondence 1928–1945* (Bodley Head: London, 1968); and Harold L. Ickes, *The Secret Diary of Harold L. Ickes* (3 volumes, Simon and Schuster: New York, 1953–54).
4. Recollection of Joseph L. Rauch, in Louchheim, *Insiders Speak*.
5. Burton Wheeler's memoirs provide a useful source. See Burton Kendall Wheeler, *Yankee from the West: The Candid, Turbulent Life Story of the Yankee-born U. S. Senator from Montana* (Doubleday: Garden City, New York, 1962).
6. The course of the Court fight may be followed through Freedman, *Roosevelt and Frankfurter*, Ickes, *Secret Diary*, Wheeler, *Yankee from the West* and Farley, *Jim Farley's Story*.
7. Richard Maidment offers a very positive view in his essay, 'The New Deal Court Revisited', in Stephen Baskerville and Ralph Willett (eds), *Nothing Else to Fear: New Perspectives on America in the Thirties* (Manchester University Press: Manchester, 1985). Less positive is William Leuchtenburg, *The Supreme Court Reborn: The*

Constitutional Revolution in the Age of Roosevelt (Oxford University Press: New York, 1995).

8. Stanley Vittoz, *New Deal Labor Policy and the American Industrial Economy* (University of North Carolina Press: Chapel Hill, 1987).

9. On the Roosevelt recession, see William J. Barber, *Designs within Disorder: Franklin D. Roosevelt, the Economists, and the Shaping of American Economic Policy, 1933–1945* (Cambridge University Press: Cambridge, 1996), pp. 102–15.

10. For the battle within the Administration over deficit spending, see Brinkley, *End of Reform*, pp. 64–102.

11. Fireside chat, 14 April 1938, Rosenman, *Roosevelt Papers*, 7, pp. 236–46.

12. There is a full description of this in William E. Leuchtenburg, 'Roosevelt, Norris and the "Seven Little TVAs"', in Leuchtenburg, *FDR Years*, pp. 159–95.

13. Savage, *Roosevelt: The Party Leader*, pp. 129–58 emphasizes Roosevelt's hopes of creating a progressive party. The impact of the attempted purge on the party faithful may be traced in Farley, *Jim Farley's Story*, pp. 120–50.

14. Brinkley, *End of Reform*, pp.106–36 discusses both these themes. FDR never fully supported Arnold's work as a trust-buster. See Wilson D. Miscamble, 'Thurman Arnold Goes to Washington: A Look at Antitrust Policy in the Later New Deal', *Business History Review* 56 (1982), pp. 1–15.

15. Rexford Tugwell suggested that the act had been amended out of all recognition, a clear sign of Congressional opposition. Tugwell, *Democratic Roosevelt*, pp. 464–7.

16. McElvaine, *Great Depression*, p. 308; and Harris, *Federal Art*, pp. 121–49.

17. See *Savage, Roosevelt: The Party Leader*, pp. 159–70.

18. On the wartime economy, see Peter Fearon, *War, Prosperity and Depression: The U.S. Economy 1917–45* (Philip Allen: Oxford, 1987), pp. 261–88. The significance of the changes in taxation are explored in Mark Leff, *The Limits of Symbolic Reform: The New Deal and Taxation 1933–1939* (Cambridge University Press: Cambridge, 1984), pp. 287–93.

19. James B. Atleson, 'Wartime labor regulation, the industrial pluralists, and the law of collective bargaining', in Nelson Lichtenstein and Howell John Harris (eds), *Industrial Democracy in America: The Ambiguous Promise* (Oxford University Press: New York, 1993), pp. 142–75.

20. Barber, *Designs within Disorder*, p. 153.

21. For an examination of Roosevelt's legacy to Truman, see William E. Leuchtenburg, *In the Shadow of FDR: From Harry Truman to Bill Clinton* (Cornell University Press: Ithaca, 1993).

CHAPTER 7

Conclusion

The question of what exactly was achieved by the New Deal is still a controversial one. However, few can deny that it altered the traditional attitude of Americans towards the underprivileged and the assumptions of what responsibilities the federal government had towards the individual citizen. Whereas the Republican administrations of the 1920s had been unashamedly one-interest administrations – that interest being big business – the New Deal restored the balance to some extent. Even if its action against business was more rhetorical than real, it insisted that poorer citizens had rights too. Indeed, the rhetorical castigations against those with excess wealth can be traced in Roosevelt's speeches from his campaign in 1932 through to the end of the New Deal. It created a new area of debate about political action and economic security. Long-term reforms included social security measures, economic regulation of business and investment, improvements in the rural sector and better labour legislation, including not only the guarantees of collective bargaining but also the virtual elimination of child labour and the sweatshop. Short-term relief covered millions of the most needy, and offered imaginative schemes to bolster self-respect. Of its short-term effects, the provision of that relief, and the overwhelming popular support which that accomplished, is the most significant of the New Deal's consequences. In short, the New Deal did much in terms of reform and relief and altered the role of the federal government permanently. That said, the New Deal operated consistently within the constraints of the fundamental structure of the capitalist system and never intended anything else. In many ways it illustrated the conservative function of social and economic reform. Moreover, it did not achieve the third of the goals of the New Deal – economic recovery. This, in part, was a reflection of the overriding economic orthodoxy of many New Dealers, particularly the President, and their willingness to put relief and the restoration of morale first. The sharp downturn during the Roosevelt recession marred the economic reputation of the New Deal. It was the Second World War, rather than the New Deal itself, which achieved many of the economic goals of the Administration and secured acceptance of government economic management.

The consequences did not always reflect the original intentions of the New Dealers. A historian of the CWA, for example, has emphasized how a programme devised by humanitarians keen to promote welfare had to draw upon professional bureaucratic expertise in order to implement their works programmes. 'Conceived as the compassionate, activist state, committed to social justice and social welfare, it developed into a more dispassionate service state with professional managers and accountants brought in to draw up organization charts and watch the budgets.'[1] Some of the more far-reaching legislation, such as the Wagner Act, derived not from the White House but from Congress. While support given to labour in the Wagner Act and Section 7(a) empowered union leaders, the strength of those unions owed as much to labour militancy and the creation of the CIO as it did to legislative protection. Although many employers resisted the legislation, some of the consequences were positive to business, resulting in more stable labour relations. Employers in labour-intensive industries in particular welcomed the creation of national standards.[2] The long-term effects in the political sphere, such as the enhanced power of the executive, the creation of a permanent government role in agriculture, even the eventual turn to deficit spending, were a consequence of events and not of long-term planning. The steady transformation of New Deal liberalism identified by Alan Brinkley, from a critique of modern capitalism to 'a set of liberal ideas essentially reconciled to the existing structure of the economy and committed to using the state to compensate for capitalism's inevitable flaws',[3] based around the use of fiscal policy, evolved during the 1930s and well away from the White House. Some of the longest-lasting changes brought about by the New Deal were not those planned and presented to Congress, but by-products of an ambitious programme encompassing all areas of political life.

Thus, for example, the relationship between federal and state governments changed irrevocably. Although still capable of acting as a powerful obstacle to the full implementation of New Deal reforms, the states lost much of their cherished independence, relying upon the federal government for funds and having to acknowledge and participate in far-reaching programmes of reform. This, however, was a reflection of

the New Deal's need to operate through the states both for sound practical reasons (the need to create a large bureaucracy virtually overnight)
and also for constitutional practice. The enhanced power of the presidency, as reflected in the sweeping powers delegated to the President in
much of the New Deal legislation, was a necessary response to a rapidly-
changing crisis, but when married to the inevitable accretion of power to
the President in wartime, transformed the executive into an imperial
presidency. The sheer multiplication of work associated with the White
House necessitated executive reorganization, and if Roosevelt was unable to secure his full proposals, later inhabitants of the White House
would build upon his achievements to forge an effective presidential
office.

This may be an appropriate point at which to consider the significance
of President Franklin D. Roosevelt to the New Deal. While in the
immediate aftermath of the New Deal its policies and significance were
largely viewed through the prism of the Roosevelt presidency, more
recent studies have tended to place him in a less central role. Discussions
of the philosophy underpinning the New Deal reforms have examined
broader issues to do with the nature of the state, the evolution in
liberalism, the relationship between government and business, the New
Deal as in many ways the epitome of a new, more modern approach to
business and capitalism. In this context, Roosevelt's role is inevitably
lessened. Similarly, the emphasis upon the complex multi-faceted
achievements of the New Deal, concentrating upon the different layers
of experience and administration, cannot justify the presence of
Roosevelt at centre stage. The New Deal was put into place by a host
of talented individuals.

It is clear that the President himself did not have a clearly articulated
view of a political philosophy; he was, in many ways, a half-hearted
reformer, still clinging to outmoded ideas like a balanced budget in the
face of experience. He was a greater politician than he was a reformer,
and it was in the field of politics that he seemed happiest (even if he made
some notable errors, such as the Supreme Court fight and the 1938 attempted purge). What has sometimes been called a 'broker state' might
be less charitably described as a vain effort to win the support of all
groups. The coalition which ultimately united behind him was in many
ways alien to his own social and political roots in rural New York state
and rural Georgia. His commitment was to politics and success as much
as, if not more than, social justice and long-term reform. This is apparent

in the way in which, despite his own personal support for legislation against the poll tax and lynching, he would never throw his political weight behind measures so guaranteed to alienate the Southern supporters of the Democratic Party. He certainly kept his own opinions close to his chest, often appearing to agree with sharply differing views on a particular topic, and often infuriating his speechwriters and advisers by a request to weave together two opposing positions. Eleanor Roosevelt justified this in her memoirs, explaining that because 'he disliked being disagreeable, he made an effort to give each person who came in contact with him the feeling that he understood what his particular interest was'.[4] At its most destructive, this approach encouraged competitive administration, while serving to retain the reins of power in Roosevelt's own hands.

It is, however, too easy to be dismissive or critical of Roosevelt's chameleon-like tendencies. As he reminded Rosenman,[5] in order to put any policies into effect, it was first necessary to be elected. Although he did not present a clear and coherent political philosophy at any time in his election campaigns, he had none the less expressed certain key themes, particularly in terms of the responsibility of the State to its citizens, which provided the impetus behind the New Deal. He had a tremendous ability to communicate his Administration's ideas and plans in terms accessible to, and accepted by, the American people. Above all, he was a facilitator as, through his political victories, he opened up the opportunity for relief and reform. He used his personal appeal, particularly fruitful in winning the support and confidence of the American people, to create an atmosphere in which a number of innovative and unprecedented policies could be implemented. That appeal had limits: when it appeared as though he was threatening the constitutional structure of the United States, he soon encountered obstacles. Yet, he was none the less the only president able to break the hallowed two-term tradition. Many of the changes with which he is associated, not least the vastly enhanced power of the presidency, owe as much to his wartime leadership as to the New Deal itself. However, while the shape of the New Deal, and its implementation on the ground, owed more to the thousands of New Dealers than it did to Roosevelt, the opportunity to implement such policies, the popular acceptance of massive change, is impossible to envisage without the role of a Roosevelt-type figure. Moreover, his humanitarian leanings are apparent in his unwillingness to tolerate suffering and need on the scale in which he encountered it, first in New York and then in the nation as a whole. Roosevelt persuaded the American people to accept the basic principle of collective responsibility for society, just as he was to guide the United States towards the assumption of world leadership which it had rejected in the 1920s. He was, in many ways, the 'first modern President'.

Although the New Deal effectively ended in the late 1930s, and President Roosevelt himself died in 1945, its impact upon the United States is reflected in the extent to which its legacies continued well into the post-war period. An important element in the continuation of reform was the liberal Supreme Court which emerged during the Roosevelt era. The new Democratic coalition continued into the post-war period and political debate continued to centre around the agenda raised by the New Dealers. This is not to say, however, that the liberal order simply continued to consolidate the New Deal agenda. One important area of increasing significance was that of racial equality and civil rights – two issues which Roosevelt's Democratic Party never dared to discuss.

Roosevelt's successors, many of whom had served under the President, continued to draw upon his legacy, while at the same time seeking to establish their own political identity.[6] When exactly did the New Deal order come to an end? There is an argument for dating its demise in the late 1960s. Lyndon Johnson, himself a member of the New Deal Congress, instituted the last of the great reform programmes, the Great Society, during his Presidency. Yet, at the same time, the Vietnam War, which shifted attention away from domestic to foreign issues, brought an end to the liberal consensus in American politics as well as in New Deal historiography. The end of the post-war affluence contributed to the decline of the preoccupation with reform. It is possible to trace continued elements of the New Deal order beyond the late 1960s, however. In an influential book, Steve Fraser and Gary Gerstle maintain that it was when Ronald Reagan assumed office in January 1981 that 'an epoch in the nation's political history came to an end'.[7]

In an earlier chapter, the effect of the Depression upon the United States was placed in a comparative perspective, in relation to the other two leading industrial powers, Great Britain and Germany. The significance of the New Deal can also be understood by adopting a comparative approach to its policies, achievements and limitations. The case of Great Britain might appear to suggest that the New Deal was irrelevant to the task of economic recovery. The British Government took a remarkably non-interventionist approach to the issue of economic recovery, which none the less came far sooner in Great Britain than in the United States. The Labour Government of Ramsey MacDonald, like that of Herbert Hoover, held to the principle of a balanced budget and also sought to maintain the value of sterling against gold and the dollar. In order to achieve this, MacDonald and his Chancellor of the Exchequer were prepared to cut the level of unemployment benefit, a policy that was indeed implemented after the Labour Cabinet had split on the issue, to be replaced by a new coalition National Government. London did not pursue a reform agenda on the lines of the New Deal, despite the urgings of politicians such as David Lloyd George. However, if we look beyond the immediate policies, we can see certain similarities. First, the British Government engaged in devaluation; in September 1931 the pound was forced off the gold standard, and by 1932 had lost roughly a quarter of its value against the dollar, trading at $3.50. It was this move away from the gold standard which probably did most to aid economic recovery in Great Britain, as it allowed the introduction of cheap credit and protectionism, including the protection and subsidy of agriculture; but little was done to address the rapid increase in unemployment. However, the British had experienced high levels of unemployment throughout the 1920s and it was also highly regionalized, by industry and geographical area. Despite this high unemployment and continued decline in foreign trade, the British economy showed signs of recovery from late 1932. Consumer demand was buoyant, as those in work enjoyed an improvement in their standard of living, money was cheaper to borrow and the price of imports fell. A very strong housing sector, helped by government assistance, and the growth in 'new' industries, such as vehicles and electrical goods, stimulated economic growth. In the period 1929–37 the British Gross National Product rose by 18 per cent while that in the United States rose by only 6 per cent.

However, there are some important qualifications to make. First, while the British economy showed signs of recovery in excess of that enjoyed by the United States, it should be remembered that the measure of growth was from a lower base. The British economy had been comparatively depressed in the 1920s, with a considerable underlying rate of unemployment and decline in many traditional industries. It is in part because the British economy started from a lower base that, first, its fall in 1929–32 was less dramatic and second, the partial improvement in the 1930s was politically acceptable. Indeed, the areas of growth during the 1930s were the very ones which had sustained the boom in the United

States during the 1920s – building, electricity and automobiles. Moreover, it was possible to pursue sectional recovery because of the existence
of a strong social security state. Those out of work might experience a
rapid drop in income, but the existence of the unemployment benefit and
functioning Poor Law for those out of work, together with the health and
old age insurance schemes for those unable to work, provided a safety
net of the kind which was only put in place in the United States by the
New Deal.

At first sight, Germany appears to demonstrate the advantages of the
very approach which the Roosevelt administration so resolutely resisted:
outright deficit spending by the government, coupled with a vigorous
expansionist philosophy. Hitler seized absolute power the day after
Roosevelt's First Inaugural, and compared with the American President,
his record was far more impressive. When he came to power, unemployment stood at over six million, by January 1936 this had already been
reduced to under three million and by January 1939 it stood at only
300,000 – a figure which amounted technically to full employment. Later
that year there was even a shortage of labour. This had been achieved
through a massive programme of government spending on infrastruc-
ture, transportation and rearmament. Industrial production nearly
doubled between 1933 and 1938. However, the costs of this apparent
success should be borne in mind. In order to achieve such economic
recovery, Germany, under Hitler's guidance, had abolished the political
and economic rights of workers, enlisting them in a Nazi-dominated
'German Labour Front' and subjecting them to wage, price and mobility
controls. Moreover, political participation had also been destroyed. The
massive expansion of the German economy had been achieved at the cost
of political and economic freedom. Furthermore, the need to compensate
for the massive deficits thus incurred, while supplying the raw materials
in very short supply, dictated a policy of aggressive German expansion.
Economic success had been achieved at the cost of political freedom and
international peace.[8]

In the course of the 1930s, therefore, the United States constructed a
partial welfare state of the kind which allowed the British Government to
follow a non-interventionist policy through the Depression. It also
retained democratic capitalism, although not achieving such strong recovery as the German dictatorship. The consequences of the New Deal
were both more widespread and more permanent than the changes
introduced in its two main economic rivals. This is, in part, because so

many of the New Deal's achievements amounted to a 'catching-up' exercise, putting in place financial controls, labour legislation and welfare provision which already existed in other industrialized nations. Democratic capitalism remained in place because the vast majority of Americans, including those in the Administration, never anticipated or considered its removal. As Ellis Hawley has persuasively argued, the Administration's half-hearted pursuit of economic policy, be it central planning or trust-busting, although economically ineffective, had positive political effects.[9] This approach reflected American public opinion, which wanted to enjoy the benefits of big business but also cherished the opportunity implicit in the old competitive order. The continued significance of the New Deal agenda in American politics after the 1930s demonstrates the extent to which it had restructured liberal thought in the United States.

Notes

1. Schwartz, *The Civil Works Administration*, p. 71.
2. Gordon, *New Deals*; and Stanley Vittoz, *New Deal Labor Policy and the American Industrial Economy* (The University of North Carolina Press: Chapel Hill, 1987), pp. 169–70.
3. Brinkley, *End of Reform*, p. 6.
4. Eleanor Roosevelt, *This I Remember* (Hutchinson: London, 1950).
5. Rosenman, *Working with Roosevelt*, p. 41.
6. See Leuchtenburg, *In the Shadow of FDR*.
7. Steve Fraser and Gary Gerstle, *The Rise and Fall of the New Deal Order, 1930–1980* (Princeton University Press: Princeton, New Jersey, 1989), p. ix.
8. See Dewey, *War and Progress* on Great Britain. On Germany, see Berghahn, *Modern Germany*; and R. J. Overy, *The Nazi Economic Recovery, 1932–1938* (Macmillan: London, 1982).
9. Ellis Hawley, *The New Deal and the Problem of Monopoly: A Study in Economic Ambivalence* (Princeton University Press: Princeton, 1966).

Suggestions for Further Reading

There is a vast literature on the New Deal, and in this selective guide I shall concentrate upon the most important works. Unfortunately there is insufficient space to discuss the very fruitful, but less accessible, material available in academic journals and unpublished theses. New monographs are published regularly, as are more detailed studies, often on a city or state basis, of developments during the New Deal years.

Perspectives on the New Deal have changed tremendously since the late 1970s when I first began teaching the subject. From an early emphasis on the administration in Washington, the politics of the Roosevelt administration and a focus on the role of the President himself, there has developed a broader approach to the New Deal period, emphasizing the work of the myriad administrators comprising the New Deal on one hand, and the impact of the New Deal upon the American people and popular culture on the other. This change of emphasis is apparent if one compares two general studies of the New Deal, published nearly thirty years apart: William Leuchtenburg, *Franklin D. Roosevelt and the New Deal 1932–1940* (Harper and Row: New York, 1963); and Anthony J. Badger, *The New Deal: The Depression Years, 1933–1940* (Macmillan: London, 1989). Leuchtenburg is an American historian, writing as a 'survivor' of the New Deal; although critical of many aspects of the Roosevelt administration, he none the less emphasizes the positive aspects of the New Deal's achievements. His treatment is chronological, with occasional chapters on international affairs; his main, though not exclusive, focus is on events in Washington DC. He sees FDR as central to the New Deal, as his book title suggests. Badger is a British historian, drawing upon the wealth of research done in the intervening period. Adopting a thematic approach, his emphasis is on the consequences and methods of the New Deal, rather than concentrating predominantly on the intentions and process of policy formation. FDR plays a far less significant role. Leuchtenburg has also published a number of articles and given many papers and lectures on the New Deal. A selection of the most significant, considerably modified and extended to incorporate new scholarship, are usefully compiled in two collections, *The Supreme Court Reborn: The Constitutional Revolution in the Age of Roosevelt* (Oxford University Press: New York, 1995) and *The FDR Years: On Roosevelt and his Legacy* (Columbia University Press: New York, 1995) He has also written a study of the successors to Roosevelt, *In the Shadow of FDR: From Harry Truman to Bill Clinton* (Cornell University Press: Ithaca, 1993).

A slightly older, but still useful study, is the three-volume work by Arthur Meier Schlesinger Jr, *The Age of Roosevelt* (3 volumes, Heinemann: London, 1957–61). This is a classic expression of liberal historiography and contains a clear assumption that there were two New Deals. Paul Conkin, *The New Deal* (Routledge: London, 1968) and the introduction to Howard Zinn (ed.), *New Deal Thought* (Bobbs-Merrill: New York, 1966) provide helpful interpretations from a New Left perspective. In addition, there are a number of volumes bringing together a series of articles on different aspects of the New Deal, including Alonzo L. Hamby (ed.), *The New Deal: Analysis and Interpretation* (2nd edition, Longman: New York, 1981), Stephen Baskerville and Ralph Willett (eds), *Nothing Else to Fear: New Perspectives on America in the Thirties* (Manchester University Press: Manchester, 1985), John Braeman, Robert Bremner and David Brody (eds), *The New Deal, vol. I: The National Level* (Ohio State University Press: Columbus, 1975), and Heinz Ickstadt, Rob Kroes and Brian Lee (eds), *The Thirties: Politics and Culture in a Time of Broken Dreams* (Free University: Amsterdam, 1987).

To set the New Deal in the context of the entire interwar period, see Gerald D. Nash, *The Great Depression and World War II : Organizing America, 1933–1945* (St. Martin's Press: New York, 1979) and Michael E. Parrish, *Anxious Decades: America in Prosperity and Depression, 1920–1941* (W. W. Norton and Co: New York, 1992). For accounts of the Hoover presidency, including discussion of whether Hoover pre-empted some of the New Deal policies, see Albert U. Romasco, *The Poverty of Abundance: Hoover, the Nation and the Depression* (Oxford University Press: New York, 1965). There are some helpful essays in Martin L. Fausold and George T. Mazuzan (eds), *The Hoover Presidency: A Reappraisal* (State University of New York Press: Albany, 1974). Joan Hoff Wilson, *Herbert Hoover: Forgotten Progressive* (Little, Brown: Boston, 1975) provides a sympathetic treatment of Hoover. For his role in the 1920s, see also Ellis W. Hawley, 'Herbert Hoover, the Commerce secretariat and the Vision of an "Associative State", 1921–28', *Journal of American History* 41 (1974) pp. 116–40.

There are a number of works written on the Depression and the economics of the New Deal. For a useful, readable and fairly straightforward account of where it all began, see J. K. Galbraith, *The Great Crash 1929* (Penguin: London, 1977). General studies of the entire interwar period, both written in an accessible style, are Jim Potter, *The American Economy Between the World Wars* (Macmillan: London, 1985) and Peter Fearon, *War, Prosperity and Depression: The U.S. Economy 1917–45* (Philip Allen: Oxford, 1987). Michael A. Bernstein, *The Great Depression: Delayed recovery and economic change in America, 1929–1939* (Cambridge: Cambridge University Press, 1987) provides a detailed study of both the events and the historiography. For the international context and comparison, see Dietmar Rothermund, *The Global Impact of the Great Depression 1929–1939* (Routledge: London, 1996), which emphasizes the impact on developing countries, and Kim Qualie Hill, *Democracies in Crisis: Public Policy Responses to the Great Depression* (Westview Press: Boulder, 1988). C. P. Kindleberger, *The World In Depression 1929–1939* (Allen Lane: London, 1973) explains the length and severity of the world depression as a consequence of the lack of leadership in the world economy. Great Britain, although willing to exercise leadership, lacked the power to do so and the United States was unwilling to assume the responsibility. A monetary explanation for the Depression may be found in Milton Friedman and Anna Jacobson Schwartz, *A Monetary History of the United States, 1867–1960* (Princeton University Press: Princeton, New Jersey, 1963), especially Chapter 7. A contrary view, emphasizing the importance of the decline in investment and spending may be found in Peter Temin, *Did Monetary Forces Cause the Great Depression?* (Norton: New York, 1976). The same author has written *Lessons from the Great Depression* (MIT Press: Cambridge, Mass., 1989). A more detailed study of the banking crises may be found in Elmus Wicker, *The Banking Panics of the Great Depression: Studies in Monetary and Financial History* (Cambridge University Press: New York, 1996).

The experience of ordinary Americans during the Depression has been discussed in a number of contexts. On unemployment see John A. Garraty, *Unemployment in History: Economic Thought and Public Policy* (Harper and Row: New York, 1978). On radical action by the unemployed, see in particular Frances Fox Piven and Richard A.

Cloward, *Poor People's Movements: Why They Succeed and Why They Fail* (Pantheon Books: New York, 1977). Studs Terkel, *Hard Times: An Oral History of the Great Depression* (Pantheon Books: New York, 1970) provides an excellent collection of recollections by those who survived the Depression. See also Robert S. McElvaine, *The Great Depression: America 1929–41* (Times Books: New York, 1984) and the same author's *Down and Out in the Great Depression: Letters from the Forgotten Man* (University of North Carolina Press: Chapel Hill, 1983) which is particularly perceptive on how the ordinary American experienced the Depression and the New Deal. To understand the popular culture of the period, there is no better way than to look at its products and components. The number of films released by Hollywood during the 1930s is immense, and many of them were of a romantic or escapist form, but there are some which reflect aspects of New Deal culture. McElvaine has a perceptive discussion on this theme. See also Andrew Bergman, *We're in the Money: Depression America and its Films* (New York University Press: New York, 1971). On the blues, see Paul Oliver, *Blues Fell This Morning: Meaning in the Blues* (Cambridge University Press, Canto edition: Cambridge, 1994).

The New Deal owed much of its inspiration to the individuals involved within it. There are many memoirs and biographies of the main participants, including, of course, Roosevelt himself. Frank B. Freidel has written several volumes of biography, of which the most significant for a study of the New Deal are *Franklin D. Roosevelt: Launching the New Deal* (Little, Brown: Boston, 1973) and *Franklin D. Roosevelt: The Triumph* (Little, Brown: Boston, 1956). James MacGregor Burns criticizes FDR for putting short-term political gain ahead of long-term reform in *Roosevelt: The Lion and the Fox* (Harcourt, Brace: New York, 1956). Kenneth S. Davis, *FDR* (3 vols, Random House: New York, 1972–86) has so far reached 1937 in his study of the President's life. Several of these biographies are as much about the New Deal as they are about FDR, reflecting an assumption that FDR and the New Deal were essentially one and the same. Eleanor Roosevelt wrote a number of volumes of autobiography of which the most relevant for the New Deal years is *This I Remember* (Harper and Row: New York, 1949). Raymond Moley, *After Seven Years* (Harper and Brothers: New York, 1939) is critical of the New Deal. Frances Perkins, *The Roosevelt I Knew* (Viking Press: New York, 1946) and Rexford Tugwell, *The Democratic Roosevelt* (Doubleday: Garden City, New York, 1957) are far more positive. On the political side of Roosevelt's presidency, James A. Farley, *Jim Farley's Story: The Roosevelt Years* (McGraw-Hill: New York, 1948), is a useful source, although it should be remembered that Farley fell out with Roosevelt towards the end of the second term. There is a growing literature about Eleanor Roosevelt, to add to her own reminiscences, notably Tamara K. Hareven, *Eleanor Roosevelt: An American Conscience* (Da Capo Press: New York, 1975); and Joan Hoff-Wilson and Marjorie Lightman (eds), *Without Precedent: The Life and Career of Eleanor Roosevelt* (Indiana University Press: Bloomington, 1984). Max Freedman (ed.), *Roosevelt and Frankfurter: Their Correspondence 1928–1945* (Bodley Head: London, 1968) is a useful source, particularly for legal and consti-tutional issues. On this, see also B. A. Murphy, *The Brandeis-Frankfurter Connection: The Secret Political Activities of Two Supreme Court Justices* (Oxford University Press: New York, 1982). The edited diaries of Harold Ickes, Harold L. Ickes, *The Secret Diary of Harold L. Ickes* (3 vols, Simon and Schuster: New York, 1953–54) provide an idiosyncratic view of the development of the New Deal. See also Michael E. Parrish, *Felix Frankfurter and his Times: The Reform Years* (The Free Press: New York, 1982); and Graham White and John Maze, *Harold Ickes of the New Deal: The Private Life and Public Career* (Harvard University Press: Cam-bridge, Mass., 1985). Ickes's big rival, Harry Hopkins, has left only memoirs of the wartime years, but his New Deal contribution may be explored through Searle F. Charles, *Minister of Relief: Harry Hopkins and the Depression* (Syracuse University Press: Syracuse, New York, 1963). Further biographies of use to the historian of the New Deal are John Kennedy Ohl, *Hugh S. Johnson and the New Deal* (Northern Illinois Press: DeKalb, 1985); Edward L. and Frederick H. Schapsmeier, *Henry A. Wallace of Iowa: The Agrarian Years, 1910–1940* (Iowa State University Press: Ames, 1968) and Bernard Sternsher, *Rexford Tugwell and the New Deal* (Rutgers University Press: New Brunswick, New Jersey, 1964). For an account of someone who was important for the New Deal, although not a member of the Administration, see Joseph J. Huthmacher, *Senator Robert F. Wagner and the Rise of Urban Liberalism* (Atheneum: New York, 1971). More difficult to ascertain are the ideas and opinions of 'second rank' New Deal administrators. A series of recollections have been collected in Katie Louchheim (ed.), *The Making of the New Deal: The Insiders Speak* (Harvard University Press: Cambridge, Mass., 1983). Although written long after the event, the book conveys the atmosphere of Washington DC during the 1930s. Of particular interest to an understanding of the evolution of the Social Security Act is Thomas H. Eliot, *Recollections of the New Deal: When the People Mattered* (Northeastern University Press: Boston, 1992).

A useful source for understanding the formation of economic policy during the New Deal is John Morton Blum, *From the Morgenthau Diaries, vol. 1: Years of Crisis, 1928–1938* (Houghton Mifflin: Boston, 1959). Ellis Hawley explains the apparent paradox between political success and economic failure in *The New Deal and the Problem of Monopoly: A Study in Economic Ambivalence* (Princeton University Press: Princeton, 1966). Albert U. Romasco has has also written a helpful survey of the New Deal, *The Poverty of Abundance: Hoover, the Nation, the Depression* (Oxford University Press: New York, 1965) and *The Politics of Recovery: Roosevelt's New Deal* (Oxford University Press: New York, 1983). For more detailed studies, see Theda Skocpol, 'Political response to Capitalist crisis: Neo-Marxist Theories of the State and the Case of the New Deal', *Politics and Society* 10 (1980), pp. 155–201, Theda Skocpol and Kenneth Finegold, 'State Capacity and Economic Intervention in the early New Deal', *Political Science Quarterly* 97 (1982), pp. 255–79 and also, Kenneth Finegold and Theda Skocpol, *State and Party in America's New Deal* (University of Wisconsin Press: Madison, Wisconsin, 1995). Two more specific aspects of financial policy are treated in Michael E. Parrish, *Securities Regulation and the New Deal* (Yale University Press: New Haven 1970) and Mark Leff, *The Limits of Symbolic Reform: The New Deal and Taxation 1933–1939* (Cambridge University Press: Cambridge, 1984). Banking reform is considered in Helen M. Burns, *The American Banking Community and New Deal Banking Reforms, 1933–1935* (Greenwood Press: Westport, Connecticut, 1974). A useful examination of the National Recovery Administration in the context of corporatism may be found in Donald R. Brand, *Corporatism and the Rule of Law: A Study of the National Recovery Administration* (Cornell University Press: Ithaca, 1988). He suggests that too strong an emphasis upon corporatism is misleading and also criticizes the pluralist explanation of the NRA. Another assessment of the NRA is provided in Michael M. Weinstein, *Recovery and Redistribution under the NIRA* (North-Holland: Amsterdam, 1980). Alan Brinkley, *The End of Reform: New Deal Liberalism in Recession and War* (Alfred A. Knopf: New York, 1995) examines changes in New Deal liberalism during the period 1936–45 and suggests that one element of this was an emphasis on the importance of consumption and a move away from an overtly hostile approach to business. Colin Gordon, *New Deals: Business, Labor, and Politics in America, 1920–1935* (Cambridge University Press: New York, 1994) suggests that many New Deal policies had precedents in the 1920s and that elements of the New Deal grew from a search for competitive order in the economy. William J. Barber has traced the changing opinions of economists and their roles in government policy in two perceptive studies, *From New Era to New Deal: Herbert Hoover, the Economists, and American Economic Policy, 1921–1933* (Cambridge University Press: Cambridge, 1985) and *Designs within Disorder: Franklin D. Roosevelt, the Economists, and the Shaping of American Economic Policy, 1933–1945* (Cambridge University Press: Cambridge, 1996).

Agriculture was very significant to the New Dealers. Val I. Perkins, *Crisis in Agriculture: The Agricultural Adjustment Administration and the New Deal 1933* (University of California Press: Berkeley, 1969) is the best study of that particular agency. T. Saloutos, *The American Farmers and the New Deal* (Iowa State University Press: Ames, 1982) and Gilbert C. Fite, *American Farmers: The New Majority* (Indiana University Press: Bloomington, 1981) both provide overviews. An excellent study of the FSA may be found in Sidney Baldwin, *Poverty and Politics: The Rise and Decline of the Farm Security Administration* (University of North Carolina Press: Chapel Hill, 1968). On the role of experts within the agricultural policy, see Richard S. Kirkendall, *Social Scientists and Farm Politics in the Age of Roosevelt* (University of Missouri Press: Columbia, 1966). The particular problems of the South are explored in Paul E. Mertz, *New Deal Policy and Southern Rural Poverty* (Louisiana State University Press: Baton Rouge, 1978); Donald H. Grubbs, *Cry from the Cotton: The Southern Tenant Farmers' Union and the New Deal* (University of North Carolina Press: Chapel Hill, 1971); and David E. Conrad, *The Forgotten Farmers: The Story of Sharecroppers in the New Deal* (University of Illinois Press: Urbana, 1965). Anthony J. Badger explores the interaction between national policy and local implementation in *Prosperity Road: The New Deal, Tobacco and North Carolina* (University of North Carolina Press: Chapel Hill, 1980). Donald Worster, *Dustbowl: The Southern Plains in the 1930s* (Oxford University Press: New York, 1979) provides an excellent study of the impact of the drought. On conservation, see John A. Salmond, *The Civilian Conservation Corps, 1933–1942: A New Deal Case Study* (Duke University Press: Durham, North Carolina, 1964), and Philip Selznick, *TVA and the Grass Roots: A Study in the Sociology of Formal Organization* (University of California Press: Berkeley, 1949).

On labour, Milton Derber and Edwin Young (eds), *Labor and the New Deal* (University of Wisconsin Press: Madison, 1957) contains a collection of articles. Two studies by Irving Bernstein, *Turbulent Years: A History of the American Worker, 1933–1941* (Houghton Mifflin: Boston, 1970) and *The New Deal Collective Bargaining Policy* (University of California Press: Berkeley, 1950) are also to be recommended. Sidney Fine, *The Automobile under the Blue Eagle: Labor, Management and the Automobile Manufacturing Code* (University of Michigan Press: Ann Arbor, 1963) provides a useful study of one industry. Stanley Vittoz, *New Deal Labor Policy and the American Industrial Economy* (University of North Carolina Press: Chapel Hill, 1987) argues against the idea that labour policy represented a clear continuity in 'taming' unions but rather the normal mixture of political expediency and interest brokering.

A number of studies have recently been published on the various agencies of the New Deal. On FERA see William R. Brock, *Welfare, Democracy and the New Deal* (Cambridge University Press: Cambridge, 1988). In *The Civil Works Administration, 1933–1934: The Business of Emergency Employment in the New Deal* (Princeton University Press: Princeton, 1984) Bonnie Fox Schwartz argues that the demise of this short-lived agency was not simply in response to the mounting costs, which attracted the opposition of fiscal conservatives, but also the ambivalence of social workers to the provision of federal employment on a large scale, undermining the traditional emphasis upon the means test, individual clients and case work. There is no comprehensive study of the WPA. On the Social Security Act, the best general study is R. Lubove, *The Struggle for Social Security, 1900–1935* (Harvard University Press: Cambridge, Mass., 1968) and, for a broader perspective, James T. Patterson, *America's Struggle Against Poverty, 1900–1980* (Harvard University Press: Cambridge, Mass., 1981). Two accounts by participants in the formulation and implementation of the legislation are E. E. Witte, *The Development of the Social Security Act* (University of Wisconsin Press: Madison, 1962) and A. J. Altmeyer, *The Formative Years of Social Security* (University of Wisconsin Press: Madison, 1966).

Many imaginative schemes catering for writers, artists and actors were developed during the New Deal, and a number of studies reflect this. Barbara Melosh, *Engendering Culture: Manhood and Womanhood in New Deal Public Art and Theatre* (Smithsonian: Washington DC, 1991) is to be recommended, as is Richard McKinzie, *The New Deal for Artists* (Princeton University Press: Princeton, 1973) and Jonathan Harris, *Federal Art and National Culture: The Politics of Identity in New Deal America* (Cambridge University Press: Cambridge, 1995). The last book draws upon theories of the state, cultural production and ideology to examine the significance and meaning of the visual art produced under the New Deal. A recent book published by the National Archives in conjunction with an exhibition on the topic, and well illustrated, is Bruce I. Bustard, *A New Deal for the Arts* (Washington DC, National Archives, 1997).

There is a rich and growing literature on the position of women in the New Deal. Susan Ware, *Beyond Suffrage: Women and the New Deal* (Harvard University Press: Cambridge, Mass., 1981) argues that there was a distinct women's network in the New Deal. The same author has also written *Holding their Own: American Women in the Twentieth Century* (G. K. Hall: Boston, Mass., 1982) and *Partner and I: Molly Dewson, Feminism and New Deal Politics* (Yale University Press: New Haven, 1987). For a general history of women, see C. Bolt, *Feminist Ferment* (UCL Press: London, 1995). For a broader perspective in which to locate developments during the New Deal, a good source is W. H. Chafe, *The American Woman: Her changing social, economic and political roles, 1920–1970* (Oxford University Press: New York, 1972). For the interwar period as a whole, see Lois Scharf and Joan M. Jensen (eds), *Decades of Discontent: The Women's Movement, 1920–40* (Greenwood Press: Westport, Connecticut, 1983). The debate over whether to focus on an Equal Rights Amendment or protective legislation for women and children is explored in Susan D. Becker, *The Origins of the Equal Rights Amendment: American Feminism between the Wars* (Greenwood Press: Westport, Connecticut, 1981). See also Lois Scharf, *To Work and to Wed: Female Unemployment, Feminism and the Great Depression* (Greenwood Press: Westport, Connecticut, 1980).

Some of the studies concentrate upon prominent women, such as the works citied earlier on Eleanor Roosevelt and those by Susan Ware. Others, however, seek to explore the fate and status of ordinary women and here the tone is less congratulatory, with the emphasis upon how welfare programmes treated women. The move away from an emphasis upon the protection of women, particularly mothers, and the consequent strengthening of the universalist male coverage of insurance schemes under the Social Security Act is treated in Theda Skocpol, *Protecting Soldiers and Mothers: The Political Origins of Social Policy in the United States* (Harvard University Press: Cambridge, Mass., 1992). Linda Gordon writes on the same theme in *Pitied but not Entitled: Single*

Mothers and the History of Welfare 1890–1935 (The Free Press, Macmillan: New York, 1994). She emphasizes the way in which questions of power and representation shaped and limited women's access to New Deal benefits. The same author has also edited *Women, the State and Welfare* (The University of Wisconsin Press: Madison, Wisconsin, 1990). This includes a number of essays on the history and development of the United States' welfare state, although it covers a far longer period than just the New Deal.

Two classic studies on the history of African Americans are H. Sitkoff, *A New Deal for Blacks: The Emergence of Civil Rights as a National Issue. vol. 1: The Depression Decade* (Oxford University Press: New York, 1978) and Raymond Wolters, *Negroes and the Great Depression: The Problem of Economic Recovery.* (Greenwood Press: Westport, Connecticut, 1970). On African American politics, see Nancy Weiss, *Farewell to the Party of Lincoln: Black Politics in the Age of FDR* (Princeton University Press: Princeton, 1983).

Much has been written on the politics of the New Deal, particularly the role of the President, and the emergence of the new Democratic coalition. On a general note, see John M. Allswang, *The New Deal and American Politics: A Study in Political Change* (Wiley: New York, 1978). A helpful study of Congressional politics may be found in James T. Patterson, *Congressional Conservatism and the New Deal: The Growth of the Conservative Coalition in Congress, 1933–1939* (University Press of Kentucky: Lexington, 1967). The creation of the New Deal Democratic coalition is discussed in Gerald H. Gamm, *The Making of the New Deal Democrats: Voting Behavior and Realignment in Boston, 1920–1940* (University of Chicago Press: Chicago, 1989). On the same theme, see Kristi Andersen, *The Creation of a Democratic Majority, 1928–1936* (University of Chicago Press: Chicago, 1979). The relationship between FDR and the Democratic Party is explored in a sympathetic study by Sean J. Savage, *Roosevelt: The Party Leader 1932–1945* (University Press of Kentucky: Lexington, 1991). Savage argues strongly that FDR was determined to turn the Democratic party into a stong liberal and progressive party. On the other hand, James MacGregor Burns, *Roosevelt: The Lion and the Fox* (Harcourt, Brace: New York, 1956) criticizes FDR for putting short term political gains before the need to create a genuinely liberal Democratic Party.

On the administration of the New Deal, and plans for reorganization, see Barry D. Karl, *Executive Reorganization and Reform in the New Deal*

(Harvard University Press: Cambridge, Mass., 1966); Charles E. Jacob, *Leadership in the New Deal: The Administrative Challenge* (Prentice-Hall: Eaglewood Cliffs, New Jersey, 1967), and A. J. Wann, *The President as Chief Administrator: A Study of Franklin D. Roosevelt* (Public Affairs Press: Washington, 1968).

The significance of the states for the New Deal has been considered in a number of studies. The best overview is James T. Patterson, *The New Deal and the States: Federalism in Transition* (Princeton University Press: Princeton, 1969). See also A. J. Badger, 'The New Deal and the Localities', in Rhodri Jeffreys-Jones and Bruce Collins (eds), *The Growth of Federal Power in American History* (Scottish Academic Press: Edinburgh, 1983). A detailed case study may be found in Sidney Fine, *Frank Murphy: The New Deal Years* (University of Chicago Press: Chicago, 1979). The city bosses were also important, as is discussed in Lyle W. Dorsett, *Franklin D. Roosevelt and the City Bosses* (Kennikat Press: Port Washington, New York, 1977).

The task of 'selling' the New Deal to the American people is explored in detail in Betty Houchin Winfield, *FDR and the News Media* (University of Illinois Press: Chicago, 1990). See also John William Tebbel and Sarah Miles Watts, *The Press and the Presidency: From George Washington to Ronald Reagan* (Oxford University Press: New York, 1985). The strong interest in factual information is explored persuasively in William Stott, *Documentary Expression and Thirties America* (Oxford University Press: New York, 1973). See also William Alexander, *Film on the Left: American Documentary Film from 1931–1942* (Princeton University Press: Princeton, New Jersey, 1981).

An important element in considering the New Deal is also to take heed of the success – and failure – of opposition parties. On the demagogues, see T. Harry Williams, *Huey Long* (Knopf: New York, 1969); A. Brinkley, *Voices of Protest: Huey Long, Father Coughlin and the Great Depression* (Knopf: New York, 1982); and H. T. Kane, *Louisiana Hayride: The American Rehearsal for Dictatorship, 1928–40* (Pelican Publishing Company: Gretna, 1986). The flavour of right-wing opposition to the New Deal may be obtained from George Wolfskill, *The Revolt of the Conservatives: a History of the American Liberty League, 1934–1940* (Houghton Mifflin: Boston, 1962); and Herbert Hoover, *The Memoirs of Herbert Hoover: The Great Depression 1929–1941* (Hollis and Carter: London, 1953). For criticism from the left, see Daniel Aaron, *Writers on the Left: Episodes in American Literary Communism* (Columbia University

Press: New York, 1992). The Socialist Party is discussed in David A. Shannon, *The Socialist Party of America: A History* (Macmillan, New York 1955); and Frank A. Warren, *An Alternative Vision: The Socialist Party in the 1930s* (Indiana University Press: Bloomington, 1976).

Index